NEW JERSEY TEST PREP

Reading Skills Workbook

Informational Texts

Grade 4

ISBN 978-1700567932

TEST MASTER PRESS

www.testmasterpress.com

CONTENTS

INTRODUCTION
For Parents, Teachers, and Tutors

New Jersey's English Language Arts Standards

The state of New Jersey has adopted the New Jersey Student Learning Standards. These standards describe what students are expected to know. The reading standards are divided into two areas: Reading Standards for Literature and Reading Standards for Informational Text. This workbook focuses specifically on informational texts. It provides practice understanding, analyzing, and responding to a wide range of informational texts.

Types of Informational Texts

The state standards and the state tests both focus on using a broad range of challenging informational texts. Students read passages based on important disciplines like science, history, and social studies. Students also read passages with a range of formats and purposes. The passages are more complex and may include items like charts, tables, graphs, diagrams, quotations, sidebars, and photographs.

This workbook provides practice with a wide variety of passage types. It includes common passage types like articles, biographies, and opinion pieces as well as more unique types like speeches, flyers, advertisements, and interviews. Each passage also includes advanced elements, and the questions help students understand and analyze these elements. The practice sets in this book will ensure that students are able to understand and analyze all types of informational texts.

Types of Reading Comprehension Questions

The state tests require students to read informational passages and answer questions to show understanding of the text. The tests include a wide variety of questions, including technology-enhanced questions that use online features. Students will answer multiple choice questions, multiple-select questions where more than one answer is selected, text selection questions where words or sentences are highlighted, written answer questions, and graphic response questions where students complete a table, diagram, or web. This workbook provides practice with a wide range of question types, and each passage also ends with an essay question.

Preparing for the NJSLA-ELA Assessments

Students will be assessed each year by taking a set of tests known as the NJSLA English Language Arts assessments. This workbook will help students master these assessments. It will ensure that students have the ability to analyze and respond to all types of challenging informational texts, while having the strong skills needed to excel on the test.

Practice Set 1

Science Article

Ben Franklin's Experiments

Instructions

This set has one passage for you to read. The passage is followed by questions.

Read each question carefully. For each multiple choice question, fill in the circle for the correct answer. For other types of questions, follow the instructions given. Some of the questions require a written answer. Write your answer on the lines provided.

Ben Franklin's Experiments

Did you know that Benjamin Franklin was the first person from the United States to prove there is electricity in nature?

In the 1750s, Benjamin Franklin was very interested in electricity. He had been reading about electricity and trying out some experiments. In 1752, he did an experiment to show that lightning is electrical current. His son William was the only person to see the experiment.

Throughout the next hundred years, many inventors and scientists from all over the world tried to find ways to use electrical power to make light.

Benjamin Franklin was sitting in his rocking chair on the front porch of his house. It was another rainy day in June. He watched as the lightning lit up the dark sky. He followed the lightning strikes with his eyes. Over and over, the sky lit up. Benjamin was interested in storms and mostly lightning. Nothing seemed to fascinate him more.

"There has to be a way for me to see if lightning is an electrical current," he told himself. He continued to watch the storm. "I just don't know how to prove it," he admitted. "I have read so many books about it. There must be a way."

The next day Benjamin was talking to one of his friends, Joseph Priestley. Priestley also shared an interest in electricity. He was doing some experiments on lightning, too.

"There must be a way for me to test lightning and see if it is an electrical current," Benjamin said. "Do you have any ideas on how this might work?"

"Not really, Ben. But, whatever you do, be careful. Lightning can be very dangerous," Priestley warned. "Remember, each thunderstorm can make over a 100 lightning strikes a second. And each bolt gives off as much energy as a ton of dynamite!"

In a few days, there was another powerful storm. By now, Benjamin had thought of an idea. He attached a large metal key to the string of a kite. He thought that if lightning is electrical current, then something metal like a key would attract it.

Then to the end of the long string, he tied a short silk ribbon which he wound tightly around his hand. This would serve as insulation and keep him safe. If there was an electrical current and it traveled to the key, it would not travel along the silk. His friend Priestley would be happy that he took some form of precaution. Just the other day, he had warned him of the dangers of lightning.

Benjamin had wanted to use a church steeple for the experiment. It was pointed high up in the sky and was the highest thing he could think of. It was made of metal and would attract the lightning. But the church steeple in Philadelphia was being built and it was not fully finished. Benjamin was not very patient. So he decided to use a kite and the metal key instead. After all, a kite can reach high up in the sky, too.

Benjamin asked his son William to come outside with him. They watched as the strong wind tossed the kite back and forth in the air. Finally the kite soared upward into the dark sky. Benjamin waited until a large storm cloud was over the kite.

Then he touched the key for less than a second. There was an electrical spark. It was not very strong. But it was a spark.

"Sure enough. Lightning is electric current!" Ben proudly said. "I now know that electricity from the storm cloud flowed down the wet string. The electric current caused the shock. I am sure it did!"

"There is nothing else to do now, but go back into the house and write about my findings. Oh, I can't wait to tell Priestley," Benjamin told William.

"It really worked, Father. It did! Here, let me carry the kite. You're all wet. You better get in some dry clothes," William said.

"Yes, William, it did work. I am so glad you could see it, too," Benjamin replied.

Many people, including Priestley, agreed that Benjamin Franklin was lucky that he only got an electric shock from this experiment. And they also agreed that this was an important experiment. It would encourage other scientists to find ways to use electrical power to make light.

Lightning Facts

- There are over 2,000 thunderstorms going on in the world at all times.
- Each lightning flash is about three miles long. They are less than an inch wide.
- Each bolt lasts a few thousandths of a second.

Ben Franklin's Jobs

Ben Franklin had many jobs in his lifetime. Here are 10 of them:

1. Bookstore owner
2. Inventor
3. Librarian
4. Politician
5. Postmaster
6. Printer
7. Scientist
8. Soldier
9. Volunteer firefighter
10. Writer

Ben Franklin's Inventions

Ben Franklin invented many things. Here are a few of these inventions:

- Bifocals
- Glass armonica (a musical instrument)
- Lightning rod
- Swimming fins
- The Franklin stove (an iron fireplace)

1   Which sentence from the second paragraph best summarizes the main idea of the passage?

Ⓐ   *In the 1750s, Benjamin Franklin was very interested in electricity.*

Ⓑ   *He had been reading about electricity and trying out some experiments.*

Ⓒ   *In 1752, he did an experiment to show that lightning is electrical current.*

Ⓓ   *His son William was the only person to see the experiment.*

2   Read these sentences from the passage.

> **"There has to be a way for me to see if lightning is an electrical current," he told himself. He continued to watch the storm. "I just don't know how to prove it," he admitted. "I have read so many books about it. There must be a way."**

Why are these sentences important in the passage?

Ⓐ   They warn about the dangers that Franklin could face.

Ⓑ   They describe the problem that Franklin is trying to solve.

Ⓒ   They show how much can be learned from reading.

Ⓓ   They help readers imagine storms and lightning.

3   In the passage, Priestley says that each bolt "gives off as much energy as a ton of dynamite." This statement is used to show that lightning is –

Ⓐ   beautiful

Ⓑ   common

Ⓒ   powerful

Ⓓ   useful

4   Which additional detail about silk could be included in the passage to help show how the silk ribbon protected Franklin?

    Ⓐ   Silk is made by silkworms and other insects.

    Ⓑ   Silk has a smooth texture and is not slippery.

    Ⓒ   Silk is one of the strongest natural fibers.

    Ⓓ   Silk does not conduct electricity well.

5   Complete the diagram below to show all the items that were used to create Franklin's invention.

```
┌──────────────┐                    ┌──────────────┐
│              │                    │              │
│              │      ┌────────┐    │              │
│              │──────┤        ├────│              │
└──────────────┘      │Items Used in│    └──────────────┘
                      │ the Invention│
┌──────────────┐      │        │    ┌──────────────┐
│              │──────┤        ├────│              │
│              │      └────────┘    │              │
│              │                    │              │
└──────────────┘                    └──────────────┘
```

6   Which **two** of Franklin's jobs listed in the sidebar best relate to the information in the passage? Tick **two** boxes to show your choices.

☐ bookstore owner   ☐ inventor

☐ librarian   ☐ politician

☐ postmaster   ☐ printer

☐ scientist   ☐ soldier

☐ volunteer firefighter   ☐ writer

7 What is the main purpose of the photograph at the start of the passage?

    Ⓐ   It helps readers imagine the scene.

    Ⓑ   It helps explain why Franklin did his experiment.

    Ⓒ   It shows that the events took place centuries ago.

    Ⓓ   It shows how lightning forms.

8 Which feature of the key best explains why it attracted the lightning?

    Ⓐ   its small size

    Ⓑ   its ability to float

    Ⓒ   its silver color

    Ⓓ   it being made of metal

9 Read these sentences from the passage.

> **Then to the end of a long string, he tied a short silk ribbon which he wound tightly around his hand. This would serve as insulation and keep him safe.**

What might have happened if Franklin had not used the silk? Explain your answer.

_____

_____

_____

_____

_____

10 The passage describes how Franklin wanted to use a church steeple for his experiment. What **two** important features did the church steeple and the kite and key invention share that made them suitable for the experiment? List the **two** features below.

1: _____

_____

2: _____

_____

11 What happened when Franklin touched the key during the storm? Explain how this proved Franklin's theory.

_____

_____

_____

_____

_____

12 Why was Franklin's experiment important? In your answer, describe how it affected other scientists.

_____

_____

_____

_____

_____

13   What does Franklin's kite invention show about his creativity? Use **two** details from the passage to support your response.

_____

_____

_____

_____

_____

_____

14   Based on your answer to Question 13, explain how this helps explain why he invented so many things. Use **two** details from the passage to support your response.

_____

_____

_____

_____

_____

_____

15 Read the statement below.

The experiment that Franklin carried out was dangerous and it was lucky he was not injured.

Write a short essay supporting the statement above. Use **three** details from the passage to support your response.

_____

_____

_____

_____

_____

_____

_____

_____

_____

_____

_____

_____

_____

_____

_____

Practice Set 2

Biography

The Life of Walt Disney

Instructions

This set has one passage for you to read. The passage is followed by questions.

Read each question carefully. For each multiple choice question, fill in the circle for the correct answer. For other types of questions, follow the instructions given. Some of the questions require a written answer. Write your answer on the lines provided.

The Life of Walt Disney

Walt Disney was born in Chicago on December 5, 1901. He had four brothers and one sister. As a child, Walt loved drawing and cartooning. He often contributed his work to the school newspaper. He also sold his art work to neighbors for extra money.

When he left school, Walt wanted to be a newspaper artist and cartoonist. Walt's brother Roy managed to get Walt a job in an art studio. There he met Ub Iwerks, a talented and respected cartoonist. Meeting Ub would inspire Walt to continue with his art and drawing.

Walt wanted to combine his love of drawing with his newfound love of animation. He opened his own animation business. Walt and his friend Fred Harman began creating short cartoons they called "Laugh-O-Grams." They sold them to theaters and began to make some money. Walt was then able to start his own small studio to keep making his laugh-o-grams. He employed many people and also began creating longer animations based on fairy tales. However, the studio could not make enough money to stay in business. In 1923, he was forced to close the studio.

Walt moved with his brother Roy to Hollywood. With Roy and his friend Ub Iwerks, Walt started a new company called Disney Brothers' Studio. They began creating new characters. One of their finest creations was Mickey Mouse. They produced an animation featuring motion pictures and sound called *Steamboat Willie*. This cartoon was extremely popular.

The cartoon launched Mickey Mouse and he became a famous character. He remains as one of the most recognizable characters around the world. Today, he is the official mascot of The Walt Disney Company. Mickey Mouse also represents a major turning point for Walt Disney and his company. Mickey was a great success, and this led to even more. As Walt Disney has said of the success of his company, "I only hope that we don't lose sight of one thing — that it all started with a mouse."

In 1929, they created new characters such as Minnie Mouse, Donald Duck, Goofy, and Pluto. Those characters appeared in many new cartoons. In 1937, they produced the first full length animated film called *Snow White and the Seven Dwarfs*. It was very successful and they won many awards for this film.

Walt and his team would go on to make many more animated films. After 1950, he began working on famous works such as *Cinderella, Alice in Wonderland, Peter Pan, Sleeping Beauty,* and *101 Dalmatians*. In 1964, he produced *Mary Poppins*, which combined live action and animation.

Walt's characters were the inspiration behind the first Disneyland. Disneyland was a theme park for children and their families. Children could meet Disney's characters and enjoy rides there too.

Disneyland was a new idea in entertainment and a huge risk. Walt Disney described what a risk it was.

> It's no secret that we were sticking just about every nickel we had on the chance that people would really be interested in something totally new and unique in the field of entertainment.

He was also surrounded by people who did not believe it was a great idea. As he said,

> We did it in the knowledge that most of the people I talked to thought it would be a disaster – closed and forgotten within the first year.

However, Walt could not be talked out of his idea and he went ahead with Disneyland. He wanted to create the happiest place on Earth. It would be a place created for children. However, it would also be a place that would allow adults to remember the joy of childhood.

Walt's gamble paid off. The first Disneyland theme park opened in Anaheim, California, in 1955. It remains open today and has over 15 million visitors each year. Both children and adults continue to enjoy the wonders of Disneyland.

Walt Disney died in 1966. His achievements during his lifetime were truly amazing. He produced some of the most watched and loved characters and animated films.

Mickey Mouse

Mickey Mouse has appeared in over 130 films. His comic strip ran for 45 years. In 1941, his film *Lend a Paw* won an Academy Award. In 1978, he became the first cartoon character to receive a star on the Hollywood Walk of Fame. He is so well known that just the shape of his head and ears allows most people to identify him!

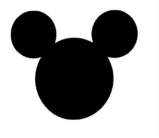

---

1   What did the success of the Laugh-O-Grams allow Walt to do?

Ⓐ   move to Hollywood

Ⓑ   quit his job

Ⓒ   start his own studio

Ⓓ   create Disneyland

2   Use details from the passage to complete the web below.

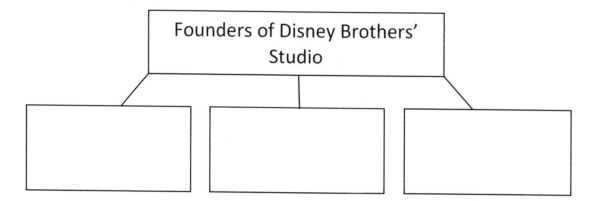

Founders of Disney Brothers' Studio

3   Read this sentence from the passage.

The cartoon launched Mickey Mouse and he became a famous character.

Which word could be used in place of *launched*?

Ⓐ   highlighted

Ⓑ   introduced

Ⓒ   sketched

Ⓓ   threw

4   Read this quote from Walt Disney.

"I only hope that we don't lose sight of one thing — that it all started with a mouse."

Which detail best shows that the importance of Mickey Mouse will not be forgotten?

Ⓐ   He is the mascot of the Walt Disney Company.

Ⓑ   He led to more characters being created, including Minnie Mouse and Pluto.

Ⓒ   A 1941 film starring Mickey Mouse won an Academy Award.

Ⓓ   Visitors to Disneyland can meet characters like Mickey Mouse.

5   Complete the table below with the two missing films.

Disney Films

Year	Film
1937	
1950	Cinderella
1951	Alice in Wonderland
1953	Peter Pan
1955	Sleeping Beauty
1959	101 Dalmatians
1964	

6   Read this quote from Walt Disney.

> *We did it in the knowledge that most of the people I talked to thought it would be a disaster – closed and forgotten within the first year.*

Despite knowing this, Walt went ahead with Disneyland. What does this suggest about Walt?

Ⓐ   He was afraid of failing.

Ⓑ   He believed in his idea.

Ⓒ   He disliked being told what to do.

Ⓓ   He was hasty and reckless.

7   The passage refers to the "wonders of Disneyland." How do these words make Disneyland seem?

Ⓐ   busy

Ⓑ   bizarre

Ⓒ   familiar

Ⓓ   magical

8   Which sentence from the information at the end on Mickey Mouse best supports the idea that Mickey Mouse is "one of the most recognizable characters around the world"?

Ⓐ   *Mickey Mouse has appeared in over 130 films.*

Ⓑ   *In 1941, his film* Lend a Paw *won an Academy Award.*

Ⓒ   *In 1978, he became the first cartoon character to receive a star on the Hollywood Walk of Fame.*

Ⓓ   *He is so well known that just the shape of his head and ears allows most people to identify him!*

9   Describe **two** ways Walt Disney shared his artwork when he was a child.

1: _____

_____

2: _____

_____

10   Determine whether each sentence below gives a fact or an opinion. Write F or O on the line to show each choice.

_____   Walt Disney was born in Chicago on December 5, 1901.

_____   One of their finest creations was Mickey Mouse.

_____   Walt and his team would go on to make many more animated films.

_____   Disneyland was a new idea in entertainment and a huge risk.

_____   The first Disneyland theme park opened in Anaheim, California, in 1955.

_____   His achievements during his lifetime were truly amazing.

11   Describe **two** ways that Walt's brother Roy influenced Walt's career.

1: _____

_____

2: _____

_____

12 Explain why the release of *Steamboat Willie* was important. Use **two** details from the passage to support your answer.

_____

_____

_____

_____

_____

13 The passage describes Mickey Mouse as a turning point for Walt Disney and his company. How is Mickey Mouse a turning point? Use **two** details from the passage to support your answer.

_____

_____

_____

_____

_____

14 Which words from Walt's quote about the risk of Disneyland best shows that the company took a huge risk?

  Ⓐ "It's no secret"

  Ⓑ "sticking just about every nickel we had"

  Ⓒ "people would really be interested"

  Ⓓ "totally new and unique"

15 What can the life of Walt Disney teach people about never giving up? Use at least **three** details from the passage to support your response.

_____

_____

_____

_____

_____

_____

_____

_____

_____

_____

_____

_____

_____

_____

_____

_____

_____

_____

Practice Set 3

Movie Review

A Review of *Inside Out*

Instructions

This set has one passage for you to read. The passage is followed by questions.

Read each question carefully. For each multiple choice question, fill in the circle for the correct answer. For other types of questions, follow the instructions given. Some of the questions require a written answer. Write your answer on the lines provided.

A Review of *Inside Out*

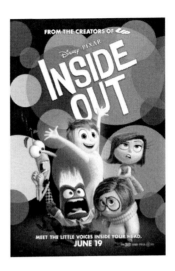

Inside Out is the perfect animated movie for young children, youth, families, and adults alike. Unlike other animated movies, *Inside Out* is not about an adventure, romance, historical fiction event, or even a trip into space. In the movie *Inside Out*, 11-year-old Riley's emotions come to life in the form of several characters called Joy, Fear, Anger, Sadness, and Disgust. Each character represents an emotion that Riley feels. As Riley struggles with a big change in her life, the characters show how her emotions change. They also show how her emotions work together to help her cope with the challenges in her life.

Plot, Setting, and Characters

When Riley's father gets a new job, her family moves from Minnesota to San Francisco. Riley faces the challenges of starting her life in a new place. Riley feels sad and angry that she left her old school, her old friends, and even her old hockey team. She doesn't like her family's "new" home, which is a little old and needs some repair, or that her father has a lot of work to do. She doesn't even like the pizza restaurant in town that gave her pizza with broccoli on it! Riley tries to adjust and be happy in her new home with the help of a set of five characters.

The movie's setting takes place mostly inside Riley's head, which is called "Headquarters." Inside Riley's head are the five characters Joy, Fear, Anger, Sadness, and Disgust. Joy is one of the main characters in *Inside Out*. She tries to help Riley feel joy in her environment. Joy is a happy and bubbly character with bright blue hair. She has a big smile and is always thinking of ways to keep Riley happy. The other characters sometimes mess up Joy's plan to help Riley stay happy. Anger is a red square-shaped character that feels angry when Riley gets annoyed or upset. Anger even has flames shoot out of his head when he gets mad. Sadness is a round blue character, with blue hair, and a frown on her face. Sadness expresses how badly Riley feels about her new home, and sometimes cries during the movie when Riley feels sadness.

Early in the plot of the movie, Riley is in her new class and the teacher asks her to stand up and introduce herself. Riley is shy and is afraid of having to talk in front of everyone. However, once she starts to talk about her old school, friends, and hockey team, she feels happy. Then she suddenly remembers how far away her old school and friends are and she becomes sad. Throughout the movie, Riley tries to be happy again with the help of her emotions that are represented by the five main characters.

Inside Riley's head, the characters Joy and Sadness get lost inside Riley's long-term memory. In the movie, Riley's long-term memory is a land full of rows of bookshelves with colored balls that represent memories.

When Joy and Sadness get "lost" Riley is confused, angry, upset, and fearful. At Headquarters, the characters Anger, Distrust, and Fear do not know how to help Riley. All five characters have to learn to work together to bring both Joy and Sadness back to Headquarters, the imaginary world inside Riley's head.

The characters Joy and Sadness who usually do not get along become friends in order to "save" Riley and her "islands." Riley's islands are several areas that are important to Riley. During *Inside Out* the safety of Riley's "islands" is risked, and Riley's happiness is threatened. Riley's islands include family, honesty, hockey, and goofiness. These four areas are very important to Riley during her life. Without honesty, family, silliness, and even hockey, Riley begins to be very sad and angry too. As Riley struggles to be happy in her new home, Anger, Fear, and Disgust are at Headquarters in an area that looks like a control room. They fight to take control of Riley's emotions and help her feel happy again. Slowly all the characters realize that they need to work together in order to help Riley feel at home again.

Learning from *Inside Out*

During the movie, we watch scenes from Riley's childhood when she was happy in Minnesota, scenes from her present life as an 11-year-old girl in her new home, and scenes from inside Riley's head. The combination of the three places helps us to understand how and why we feel emotions. While we watch *Inside Out* we learn about how memory works. We also learn about how and why we respond the way we do to different events that happen in our lives. *Inside Out* teaches us about how we feel emotions, and the psychology of the mind.

Everyone feels and expresses a wide range of emotions. *Inside Out* explores how people feel and why people feel that way.

The creators of *Inside Out* made a unique film that combines animated characters in an imaginary "mind setting" with psychology. As we watch the movie, we feel the emotions that Riley feels when she misses her old home.

Why Watch *Inside Out*?

Inside Out is an amazing film that helps bring emotions to life through "real" characters. It is also very funny when the characters interact with each other and try to help Riley. People of all ages can enjoy this film and laugh too when they watch *Inside Out.*

1   Read this sentence from the passage.

> ***Inside Out* is the perfect animated movie for young children, youth, families, and adults alike.**

What does this sentence show about the author?

Ⓐ   She has seen the movie many times.

Ⓑ   She thinks the movie is suitable for all ages.

Ⓒ   She believes the movie has an important message.

Ⓓ   She prefers animated movies over other types.

2   Which sentence from the first paragraph is a comparison? Select the **one** correct answer.

☐   *Inside Out* is the perfect animated movie for young children, youth, families, and adults alike.

☐   Unlike other animated movies, *Inside Out* is not about an adventure, romance, historical fiction event, or even a trip into space.

☐   In the movie *Inside Out*, 11-year-old Riley's emotions come to life in the form of several characters called Joy, Fear, Anger, Sadness, and Disgust.

☐   Each character represents an emotion that Riley feels.

☐   As Riley struggles with a big change in her life, the characters show how her emotions change.

☐   They also show how her emotions work together to help her cope with the challenges in her life.

3   Based on the information in paragraph 2, list **four** reasons Riley does not like her new home.

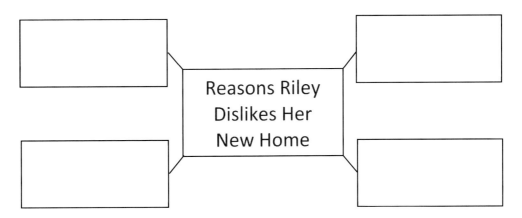

4   Read this sentence from the passage.

Joy is a happy and bubbly character with bright blue hair.

Which word means about the same as *bubbly*?

Ⓐ   cheerful

Ⓑ   loud

Ⓒ   playful

Ⓓ   talkative

5   According to the review, what represents Riley's memories?

Ⓐ   an island

Ⓑ   colored balls

Ⓒ   a control room

Ⓓ   a set of characters

6 Read this paragraph from the passage.

> **When Joy and Sadness get "lost" Riley is confused, angry, upset, and fearful. At Headquarters, the characters Anger, Distrust, and Fear do not know how to help Riley. All five characters have to learn to work together to bring both Joy and Sadness back to Headquarters, the imaginary world inside Riley's head.**

What aspect of the movie does this paragraph mainly describe?

ⓐ characters

ⓑ plot

ⓒ setting

ⓓ theme

7 The review describes the characters that represent Riley's emotions. Complete the table below by listing **two** ways each character's appearance or actions represent the emotion.

Character	Appearance or Action	Appearance or Action
Joy		
Anger		
Sadness		

8   Paragraph 4 describes how Riley stands up in class to introduce herself. Summarize the changing emotions Riley feels by completing the diagram below. State the emotion she feels and give a brief statement about why she feels that emotion. The first one has been completed for you.

```
┌─────────────────────────────────────────────┐
│                                             │
│  Emotion: shy and afraid                    │
│                                             │
│  Reason: feels nervous speaking in front of │
│  everyone                                   │
│                                             │
└─────────────────────────────────────────────┘
                      │
                      ▼
┌─────────────────────────────────────────────┐
│                                             │
│  Emotion: _____             │
│                                             │
│  Reason: _____  │
│                                             │
│  _____  │
│                                             │
└─────────────────────────────────────────────┘
                      │
                      ▼
┌─────────────────────────────────────────────┐
│                                             │
│  Emotion: _____             │
│                                             │
│  Reason: _____  │
│                                             │
│  _____  │
│                                             │
└─────────────────────────────────────────────┘
```

9   Based on the information in the section titled "Learning from *Inside Out*," list **three** things the movie teaches people about psychology.

1. _____

2. _____

3. _____

10   What are Riley's four islands? What do they represent and why are they important? Use details from the passage to support your answer.

_____

_____

_____

_____

_____

11   Read this sentence from the passage.

> **During the movie, we watch scenes from Riley's childhood when she was happy in Minnesota, scenes from her present life as an 11-year-old girl in her new home, and scenes from inside Riley's head.**

What would the comparison of Riley's current life and her life in Minnesota probably emphasize? Explain your answer.

_____

_____

_____

_____

_____

12   What does the art of the people in the passage help readers understand? In your answer, explain how it relates to the movie *Inside Out*.

_____

_____

_____

_____

_____

13 What new information is included in the last paragraph that is not described in the rest of the review? Explain your answer.

_____

_____

_____

_____

14 Why do you think the movie is titled *Inside Out*? What do you think the title of the movie refers to? Explain your answer.

_____

_____

_____

_____

15   The movie is about a girl who moves to a new place and dislikes it. This is not a unique idea, but the movie itself is unique. What makes the movie unique and different? Use at least **three** details from the passage to support your answer.

_____

_____

_____

_____

_____

_____

_____

_____

_____

_____

_____

_____

_____

_____

_____

_____

Practice Set 4

Instructional Texts

Set of Three Instructional Texts

Instructions

This set has several passages for you to read. Each passage is followed by questions.

Read each question carefully. For each multiple choice question, fill in the circle for the correct answer. For other types of questions, follow the instructions given. Some of the questions require a written answer. Write your answer on the lines provided.

Baking Bread: From Basics to Brilliance

Is there anything better than the smell of fresh-baked bread? Being able to make your own bread is a great skill to have. It is a skill that all your friends and family will appreciate. Baking basic bread uses a simple recipe and process. Once you have mastered this, then you can really start making some great creations. You can add new ingredients to make things like herb bread, bacon and cheese bread, or even chocolate and banana chip bread.

One bread that is very popular is olive bread. The salty olives add a delicious flavor that makes people want more and more. It's great as a snack or on the side of Italian meals like pastas or meatballs.

1   What is the author's overall main purpose in the second paragraph?

     Ⓐ   to encourage people to want to make olive bread

     Ⓑ   to highlight that making olive bread is simple

     Ⓒ   to explain how to best serve olive bread

     Ⓓ   to compare olive bread to other breads

2   Based on the recipe, complete the list of ingredients below.

Olive Bread Ingredients

1. Flour

2. Warm water

3. _____

4. _____

5. _____

6. _____

7. _____

3   What does the clock in Step 2 of the instructions represent?

     Ⓐ   what time of day to make the bread

     Ⓑ   how long to let the dough sit for

     Ⓒ   how much patience bakers of bread need

     Ⓓ   how long to bake the bread for

4 Look at Step 3 in the instructions. Complete the list below to describe **two** more different purposes of the arrows.

1: The arrows near the knife represent chopping the olives.

2: _____

_____

3: _____

_____

5 Which step in the instructions would be most different if you were making herb bread or bacon and cheese bread instead of olive bread? Explain how the step you have selected would be different.

_____

_____

_____

_____

_____

6 Based on the passage, how do you make bread go from "basics to brilliance"? Explain how olive bread is an example of this.

_____

_____

_____

_____

Ladder Safety

Did you know that over 50 workers are injured in ladder-related accidents in the United States every day? Most of these accidents can be prevented if people use ladders carefully and follow a few safety rules.

You or your family members probably use ladders around the home too. Ladders are useful tools that make many jobs easier. How else could you change that light bulb that is too high to reach, hang that rope swing on a high tree branch, or clean the outside of your second floor window?

The important thing when using ladders at work or at home is to be careful, avoid rushing, and make sure you are using the ladder safely.

Six Rules for Safe Ladder Use

1. Use A Ladder Of The Correct Length
2. Inspect The Ladder Carefully
3. Transport Ladder Carefully
4. Set On A Reliable Surface
5. Install The Ladder Correctly
6. Secure The Ladder At The Top

Check Also

Pay Attention To Your Health

Use A Tool Belt

Check Your Shoes

1   Read this sentence from the passage.

Did you know that over 50 workers are injured in ladder-related accidents in the United States every day?

What is the main purpose of this sentence?

Ⓐ   to describe how useful ladders are

Ⓑ   to tell how to use a ladder properly

Ⓒ   to show how dangerous ladders can be

Ⓓ   to warn people about using ladders at home

2   Read this sentence from the passage.

How else could you change that light bulb that is too high to reach, hang that rope swing on a high tree branch, or clean the outside of your second floor window?

Which term best describes these sentences?

Ⓐ   definitions

Ⓑ   examples

Ⓒ   facts

Ⓓ   instructions

3   A person using a ladder places the ladder on wet slippery tiles. Which of the safety rules is the person breaking?

☐   Rule 1   ☐   Rule 4

☐   Rule 2   ☐   Rule 5

☐   Rule 3   ☐   Rule 6

4   What does the photograph at the start of the passage show? Explain how this photograph relates to the information in the passage.

_____

_____

_____

_____

5   Look at the illustration of the person on the ladder in the instructions. How does this illustration help show why it is important to wear a tool belt? Explain your answer.

_____

_____

_____

_____

6   The passage describes how it is important to avoid rushing when using a ladder. Use details from the instructions to list **two** reasons it is important not to rush.

1: _____

_____

2: _____

_____

Finding Your Fluffy Friend

Oh no! You haven't seen your pet cat for ages and you're getting worried. What should you do? First of all, don't panic. It is common for cats to wander or explore, but they usually return home. Cats can also be very lazy. It's quite possible your cat has just found a cozy spot and is lazing away there.

So don't panic, but you can also take some simple steps to help find your fluffy friend. Here are some great tips to help get you started.

And finally, there is one very important thing you can do to make it easier for other people to help find your cat. You can make sure your name and phone number is either printed on your cat's collar, or attached to your cat's collar with a tag.

Missing cats can often be found hanging around the homes of other cats. This is usually because they are eating the other cat's food. As long as your name and number is on your cat, people can easily contact you to let you know your cat is hanging around their place.

1   What does Step 7 in the set of instructions suggest?

    Ⓐ   The cat will take a long time to find.

    Ⓑ   The cat will be happy to be home.

    Ⓒ   The cat will be found again.

    Ⓓ   The cat should be kept inside.

2   Read this sentence from the passage.

> **It's quite possible that your cat has just found a cozy spot and is lazing away there.**

Which step in the instructions has the same main idea as this sentence?

☐   Step 1   ☐   Step 5

☐   Step 2   ☐   Step 6

☐   Step 3   ☐   Step 7

☐   Step 4

3   How does the author show that there is no need to panic in the first paragraph? Use **two** details from the paragraph in your answer.

_____

_____

_____

_____

_____

4   How are the first four steps of the instructions similar? Explain your answer.

_____

_____

_____

_____

_____

5   Look at the illustrations used in the instructions. Do the illustrations make the instructions seem serious or light-hearted? Use a description of the illustrations to support your answer.

_____

_____

_____

_____

_____

6   Describe **two** things people could do to help people contact them about a lost cat. Use details from the passage and instructions in your answer.

1: _____

_____

2: _____

_____

Practice Set 5

Speech

Find What You Love

Instructions

This set has one passage for you to read. The passage is followed by questions.

Read each question carefully. For each multiple choice question, fill in the circle for the correct answer. For other types of questions, follow the instructions given. Some of the questions require a written answer. Write your answer on the lines provided.

Find What You Love
Adapted from a Speech by Steve Jobs, 2005

I am honored to be with you today at your commencement from Stanford University, one of the finest universities in the world. I never graduated from college. Truth be told, this is the closest I've ever gotten to a college graduation.

I dropped out of Reed College after the first 6 months, but then stayed around as a drop-in for another 18 months or so before I really quit. So why did I drop out?

©BlackAkaliko / Shutterstock.com

It started before I was born. My biological mother was a young, unwed college graduate student, and she decided to put me up for adoption. She felt very strongly that I should be adopted by college graduates, so everything was all set for me to be adopted at birth by a lawyer and his wife. Except that when I popped out they decided at the last minute that they really wanted a girl. So my parents, who were on a waiting list, got a call in the middle of the night asking: "We have an unexpected baby boy; do you want him?" They said: "Of course." My biological mother later found out that my mother had never graduated from college and that my father had never graduated from high school. She refused to sign the final adoption papers. She only relented a few months later when my parents promised that I would someday go to college.

And 17 years later, I did go to college. But I naively chose a college that was almost as expensive as Stanford, and all of my working-class parents' savings were being spent on my college tuition. After six months, I couldn't see the value in it. I had no idea what I wanted to do with my life and no idea how college was going to help me figure it out. And here I was spending all of the money my parents had saved their entire life. So I decided to drop out and trust that it would all work out okay.

It was pretty scary at the time, but looking back it was one of the best decisions I ever made. The minute I dropped out I could stop taking the required classes that didn't interest me, and begin dropping in on the ones that looked interesting.

It wasn't all romantic. I didn't have a dorm room, so I slept on the floor in friends' rooms. I returned Coke bottles for the 5¢ deposits to buy food with, and I would walk the 7 miles across town every Sunday night to get one good meal a week at the Hare Krishna temple. I loved it. And much of what I stumbled into by following my curiosity and intuition turned out to be priceless later on. Let me give you one example.

Reed College at that time offered perhaps the best calligraphy instruction in the country. Throughout the campus every poster, every label on every drawer, was beautifully hand calligraphed. Because I had dropped out and didn't have to take the normal classes, I decided to take a calligraphy class to learn how to do this. I learned about typefaces, about spacing, about what makes great typography great. It was beautiful, historical, artistically subtle in a way that science can't capture, and I found it fascinating.

None of this had even a hope of any practical application in my life. But 10 years later, when we were designing the first Macintosh computer, it all came back to me. And we designed it all into the Mac. It was the first computer with beautiful typography. If I had never dropped in on that single course in college, the Mac would have never had multiple typefaces or proportionally spaced fonts. And since Windows just copied the Mac, it's likely that no personal computer would have them. If I had never dropped out, I would have never dropped in on this calligraphy class, and personal computers might not have the wonderful typography that they do. Of course it was impossible to connect the dots looking forward when I was in college. But it was very, very clear looking backward 10 years later.

Again, you can't connect the dots looking forward; you can only connect them looking backward. So you have to trust that the dots will somehow connect in your future. You have to trust in something — your gut, destiny, life, karma, whatever. This approach has never let me down, and it has made all the difference in my life.

I was lucky — I found what I loved to do early in life. Woz and I started Apple in my parents' garage when I was 20. We worked hard, and in 10 years Apple had grown from just the two of us in a garage into a $2 billion company with over 4,000 employees. We had just released our finest creation — the Macintosh — a year earlier, and I had just turned 30. And then I got fired. How can you get fired from a company you started? Well, as Apple grew we hired someone who I thought was very talented to run the company with me, and for the first year or so things went well. But then our visions of the future began to diverge and eventually we had a falling out. When we did, our Board of Directors sided with him. So at 30, I was out. And very publicly out. What had been the focus of my entire adult life was gone, and it was devastating.

I really didn't know what to do for a few months. I felt that I had let the previous generation of entrepreneurs down — that I had dropped the baton as it was being passed to me. I was a very public failure, and I even thought about running away from the valley. But something slowly began to dawn on me — I still loved what I did. The turn of events at Apple had not changed that one bit. I had been rejected, but I was still in love. And so I decided to start over.

I didn't see it then, but it turned out that getting fired from Apple was the best thing that could have ever happened to me. The heaviness of being successful was replaced by the lightness of being a beginner again, less sure about everything. It freed me to enter one of the most creative periods of my life.

During the next five years, I started a company named NeXT, another company named Pixar, and fell in love with an amazing woman who would become my wife. Pixar went on to create the world's first computer animated feature film, *Toy Story*. *Toy Story* made over $350 million worldwide. Pixar is now the most successful animation studio in the world. NeXT grew to have over 500 employees. In a remarkable turn of events, Apple bought NeXT for just over $400 million. I returned to Apple, and the technology we developed at NeXT is at the heart of Apple's current renaissance. And Laurene and I have a wonderful family together.

I'm pretty sure none of this would have happened if I hadn't been fired from Apple. It was awful tasting medicine, but I guess the patient needed it. Sometimes life hits you in the head with a brick. Don't lose faith. I'm convinced that the only thing that kept me going was that I loved what I did.

You've got to find what you love. Your work is going to fill a large part of your life, and the only way to be truly satisfied is to do what you believe is great work. And the only way to do great work is to love what you do. If you haven't found it yet, keep looking. Don't settle. As with all matters of the heart, you'll know when you find it. And, like any great relationship, it just gets better and better as the years roll on. So keep looking until you find it. Don't settle.

"Let's go invent tomorrow rather than worrying about what happened yesterday."
–Steve Jobs

1   Read this sentence from the first paragraph of the speech.

I am honored to be with you today at your commencement from Stanford University, one of the finest universities in the world.

As it is used in the sentence, what does the word *finest* mean?

Ⓐ   oldest

Ⓑ   thinnest

Ⓒ   most costly

Ⓓ   highest quality

2   In paragraph 6, Steve describes his time at college as not being all romantic. Complete the diagram by listing **three** details Steve gives to show his difficulties at this time.

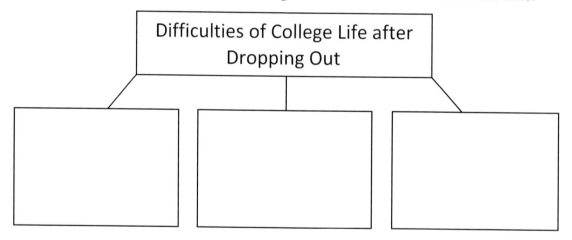

3   According to the speech, why did Steve take calligraphy courses at Reed College?

Ⓐ   He hoped to use it in his later work with computers.

Ⓑ   He was impressed by the calligraphy and curious about it.

Ⓒ   He knew the college offered the best courses in the topic.

Ⓓ   He hoped to find a way to make money while at college.

4   In which sentence from paragraph 9 does Steve show how his attitude to life has influenced him personally?

Ⓐ   *Again, you can't connect the dots looking forward; you can only connect them looking backward.*

Ⓑ   *So you have to trust that the dots will somehow connect in your future.*

Ⓒ   *You have to trust in something — your gut, destiny, life, karma, whatever.*

Ⓓ   *This approach has never let me down, and it has made all the difference in my life.*

5   Which sentence from paragraph 10 gives a sudden turning point that would probably surprise listeners?

Ⓐ   *Woz and I started Apple in my parents' garage when I was 20.*

Ⓑ   *We worked hard, and in 10 years Apple had grown from just the two of us in a garage into a $2 billion company with over 4,000 employees.*

Ⓒ   *We had just released our finest creation — the Macintosh — a year earlier, and I had just turned 30.*

Ⓓ   *And then I got fired.*

6   Choose **one** of the businesses that Steve Jobs started after leaving Apple. For the business you selected, list **two** details that show its success.

Business	Detail that Shows the Success of the Business
	1)
	2)

7   In paragraph 3, Steve describes how he was adopted by his parents. Describe **two** events that could have caused Steve to be adopted by different people.

1: _____

_____

2: _____

_____

8   Read this sentence from the speech.

> **But I naively chose a college that was almost as expensive as Stanford, and all of my working-class parents' savings were being spent on my college tuition.**

How did Steve feel about the cost of college for his parents? How did this affect his decision to drop out? Explain your answer.

_____

_____

_____

_____

_____

9 How did dropping out of Reed College give Steve freedom? Use **two** details from the passage to support your answer.

_____

_____

_____

_____

_____

10 Read this description of the calligraphy classes.

None of this had even a hope of any practical application in my life.

Did this remain true? Use **two** details from the passage to support your answer.

_____

_____

_____

_____

11 In paragraph 10, Steve describes how he came to be fired from Apple. How were his feelings about it at the time different from his feelings about it when giving the speech? Explain your answer.

_____

_____

_____

_____

_____

12 Read the quote at the end of the speech. How does this quote relate to what Steve did after being fired from Apple? Explain your answer.

_____

_____

_____

_____

_____

13   Read these statements about how Steve changed after being fired from Apple.

The heaviness of being successful was replaced by the lightness of being a beginner again, less sure about everything. It freed me to enter one of the most creative periods of my life.

How is Steve's attitude similar to how he felt after dropping out of college? Use **two** details from the passage to support your answer.

_____

_____

_____

_____

_____

14   Select the statement that best summarizes Steve's message to the audience of college graduates in the last paragraph. Select the **one** best answer.

☐   Never stop learning.

☐   Have a balanced life.

☐   Find your passion.

☐   Seek out opportunities.

☐   Work harder than those around you.

☐   Find a strong role model.

15   Steve states that it is important that people love what they do. How did loving what he did help Steve during difficult times? Use **three** details from the speech to support your answer.

_____

_____

_____

_____

_____

_____

_____

_____

_____

_____

_____

_____

_____

_____

_____

Practice Set 6

Promotional Article

Discovery Elementary's Fundraising Festival

Instructions

This set has one passage for you to read. The passage is followed by questions.

Read each question carefully. For each multiple choice question, fill in the circle for the correct answer. For other types of questions, follow the instructions given. Some of the questions require a written answer. Write your answer on the lines provided.

Discovery Elementary's Fundraising Festival

Attention all Discovery Elementary students, parents, and teachers! This weekend, our wonderful school will be holding the annual Fundraising Festival where you can play wacky games, win jaw-dropping prizes, eat delicious treats, and create memories with your friends! By joining the fun you'll be helping your school raise money that will go towards building a bright future for our community. Every dollar spent will go towards helping our school improve the way our students learn and play!

What to Expect

Discovery Elementary knows how to have fun! At the Fundraising Festival, there will be upbeat music played by student DJs, colorful decorations created by talented student artists, game booths with tons of exciting prizes, food stands with delicious snacks from around the world, a petting zoo where you can feed baby farm animals, a photo booth to capture precious memories, and even a dunk tank where you can dunk your favorite teachers in water!

When you arrive, you can exchange your cash for tokens at our token booth. Every $1 will get you 4 tokens that you can use at any game stand, activity center, or food booth. The more tokens you buy, the more fun you'll have and the more prizes you'll have the chance of taking home! You don't want to miss this Fundraising Festival!

International Delights

Do you like Italian pizza topped with gooey mozzarella cheese? What about sweet mango sticky rice from Thailand? Have you ever tasted German sausage with yellow mustard? At the Fundraising Festival, you can try food from countries all around the world that represent our student body at Discovery Elementary.

You'll have the chance to try fried ice cream from Mexico, chickpea hummus from Lebanon, chicken kebabs from Bulgaria, and much more! Of course, you'll find a few American classics like caramel-covered apples, hotdogs, and pretzels as big as your head! There will be vegetarian options, dairy-free treats, gluten free snacks, and every dish will be free of nuts. There will be something for everyone to enjoy here!

Where the Money Goes

Every dollar spent will go towards making Discovery Elementary the best grade school in the county! The student council has worked very hard to ask students, teachers, parents, and Principal Matthews what changes and improvements they would like to see in our school. The students would like to freshen up the playground with new paint and purchase a basketball hoop so we can expand our physical education. The teachers are excited about buying new laptops for the library and replacing the chalkboards with electronic whiteboards in their classrooms. The parents have requested that more fresh fruits and vegetables will be used in their children's school lunches every week. And the best suggestion of all comes from Principal Matthews. He would like to create a pet program so that every classroom has a pet mascot such as a rabbit, an iguana, or a slithery snake.

Every class could have their very own pet to share! What a wonderful idea!

Costume Contest

Dress to impress at the Fundraising Festival where an undercover team of judges will be walking around to decide who has the craziest outfit. You can go wild with crazy hairstyles, get clownish with bright and colorful clothes, transform into your favorite superhero with genuine costumes, or be artsy with face paint that shows off your imagination. Discovery Elementary has lots of creative students so expect the competition to be fierce!

Towards the end of the festival, the music will stop and Principal Matthews will get on the microphone to announce the top three winners! The third prize will be a coupon to eat lunch with your favorite teacher. The second prize will be a "no homework" pass that is good for one homework assignment in your homeroom class. The clever first prizewinner will win a pizza party for their entire class! Be creative, have fun, and you just might be a lucky winner!

We need all of you to come together for Discovery Elementary's Fundraising Festival and help our school reach its goals! Clear your schedule this Friday, May 21, so that you can join in on the fun! You can bring your parents, grandparents, siblings, cousins, or even a few friends from neighboring schools. Everyone is going to have a wonderful time and every dollar spent goes towards a great cause! Be the change you want to see in our school! We can't do it without you!

1   Read this sentence from the passage.

> **This weekend, our wonderful school will be holding the annual Fundraising Festival where you can play wacky games, win jaw-dropping prizes, eat delicious treats, and create memories with your friends!**

What does the word *jaw-dropping* mean?

Ⓐ   exciting

Ⓑ   funny

Ⓒ   scary

Ⓓ   valuable

2   What does the illustration in the first paragraph most likely represent?

Ⓐ   how long the festival has been running for

Ⓑ   how good a time people will have at the festival

Ⓒ   how the funds raised from the festival will be spent

Ⓓ   how much money the festival hopes to raise

3   Which **two** features described in "What to Expect" are present to create a fun atmosphere rather than to make money? Select the **two** best answers.

☐   upbeat music

☐   colorful decorations

☐   game booths

☐   food stands

☐   petting zoo

☐   dunk tank

4   As it is used in paragraph 2, which word means about the same as *upbeat*?

    Ⓐ   cheerful

    Ⓑ   loud

    Ⓒ   modern

    Ⓓ   original

5   Complete the table below by listing **three** more examples of countries and the food available to represent that country.

Food Available at the Festival

Country	Food
Italy	Pizza

6   Which suggestion in "Where the Money Goes" does the author seem most enthusiastic about? Select the **one** best answer.

    ☐   freshening up the playground

    ☐   purchasing a basketball hoop

    ☐   getting new laptops

    ☐   replacing the chalkboards

    ☐   having more fresh fruit and vegetables

    ☐   starting a pet program

7   Read the sentences from the passage below. Circle **three** phrases that suggest that people should be creative and have fun with the costumes.

> Dress to impress at the Fundraising Festival where an undercover team of judges will be walking around to decide who has the craziest outfit. You can go wild with crazy hairstyles, get clownish with bright and colorful clothes, transform into your favorite superhero with genuine costumes, or be artsy with face paint that shows off your imagination.

8   Which section of the passage has the purpose of summarizing the main events of the festival?

Ⓐ   What to Expect

Ⓑ   International Delights

Ⓒ   Where the Money Goes

Ⓓ   Costume Contest

9   Describe **two** ways the author makes readers feel good about spending money in the section titled "Where the Money Goes."

1: _____

_____

2: _____

_____

10   Read these sentences from the passage.

> **When you arrive, you can exchange your cash for tokens at our token booth. Every $1 will get you 4 tokens that you can use at any game stand, activity center, or food booth.**

Why are these sentences important in the passage? In your answer, tell what these sentences help readers understand about raising money.

_____

_____

_____

_____

_____

11   The section titled "International Delights" states that there is something for everyone to enjoy. How does the author support this statement? Use **two** details from the section to support your response.

_____

_____

_____

_____

_____

12   The section titled "Where the Money Goes" describes how different people have different ideas on what to spend the money on. Who wants to spend the money on technology? Explain your answer.

_____

_____

_____

_____

_____

13   Describe **two** ways the author makes readers feel important in the last paragraph.

1. _____

_____

2. _____

_____

14   Compare the prizes given for the costume contest. How is the first prize different from the second and third prizes?

_____

_____

_____

_____

_____

15   Do you think the Fundraising Festival is a clever way to raise money? Use at least **three** details from the passage to support your response.

_____

_____

_____

_____

_____

_____

_____

_____

_____

_____

_____

_____

_____

_____

_____

_____

Practice Set 7

How-To Article

How to Help the Earth Stay Healthy

Instructions

This set has one passage for you to read. The passage is followed by questions.

Read each question carefully. For each multiple choice question, fill in the circle for the correct answer. For other types of questions, follow the instructions given. Some of the questions require a written answer. Write your answer on the lines provided.

How to Help the Earth Stay Healthy

Have you ever thought about how good our planet Earth is to you? If you are sweating on a hot day, you can relax under a shady tree. You can take a sip of cool water that the rivers, streams, and lakes of our planet provide. The food you eat also comes from the Earth. And then there's everything beautiful the Earth provides like sparkling beaches, lush forests, and impressive canyons.

Unfortunately, the Earth is not as healthy as it once was. To live our lives today, we also use the Earth's resources. Coal and oil is used to power our homes and our cities. Factories all over the world produce all types of goods. This activity changes the Earth. It creates pollution, leads to global warming, and causes trash to build up in landfills.

How healthy is our planet? That's partly up to you!

It's not all bad, though. Many people today are making small changes to their lives to help the Earth. It's all about balance and making smart choices. You can enjoy all that the Earth provides, while still making small efforts to help protect the Earth.

Reduce Electricity Wastage

A lot of electricity gets wasted when things are left on when they're not in use. Get yourself in the habit of turning off lights when you leave a room and shutting off the air conditioning when you don't need it. You can also make sure you turn off the television when you're not really watching it. Many people get used to just having the television on in the background, but there's no need for this! You should also remember to shut down your computer each time you have finished using it. Many computers will stay on for a while and then shut themselves down if they're not used. People can get used to this feature and stop taking the simple step of shutting down when they're finished.

It's also important to know that many things will keep using electricity even when they're turned off. Televisions, computers, and phone chargers can stay in standby mode and keep using electricity when there's no good reason to. This can easily be prevented by turning the items off at the wall. It's an easy habit to get into and you won't even notice the difference.

With a little extra thought, you can reduce how much electricity you use every day. This means less power needs to be created and that's good for the Earth. It's also good for you because it saves you wasting money!

Keeping Cool

Air conditioners suck up the most energy in your home if you leave them on all summer long! There are many others ways you can keep cool. Buy a fan that will cool you down while watching television, reading a book, or sleeping. Fans use much less energy than air conditioners. There is also sometimes no need to cool down a whole house or a huge space. Instead, you can just cool down where you are. Small fans are great for this.

You can also stay cool without using any electricity. Open a window to allow a nice summer breeze to roll in. Fill up a spray water bottle with clean water and spray it on your face to help you cool off. To keep your body from overheating, drink lots of water during the day.

If you do decide to use your air conditioner, make sure that all of your windows or doors in the house are closed so that cool air doesn't escape and your air conditioner doesn't have to work harder.

Choose Your Appliances Wisely

We have all become used to appliances. Washing machines, microwave ovens, and even robotic vacuum cleaners all make our lives easier. You don't have to give these things up to help the Earth. You just have to think carefully about which ones to buy.

First of all, old refrigerators, vacuum cleaners, and air conditioners use up more energy than newer ones. New machines are built with saving energy in mind. If you have really old appliances, think about replacing them with new ones.

When you do buy appliances, they come with energy ratings. These tell you how efficient the items are. The Energy Star program was created by the Environmental Protection Agency to help people make smarter choices. Products that are energy efficient and good for the environment are able to display the Energy Star symbol. As a shopper, you don't need to compare numbers or check data yourself. You can simply look for products with the sticker and you will know you are making a good choice.

Appliances like washing machines or dishwashers will also have ratings telling you how much water they use. Do some research and make smart choices when you choose your appliances.

Recycle and Reuse

Paper, plastic, aluminum, and glass are all recyclable materials! That means that your paper bags, plastic cups, soda cans, and glass bottles can all be used again. When you recycle these items, they are sent to a factory that cleans them, crushes them, melts them, and makes them into new items. Recycling is amazing! The best thing is that this reduces the amount of new items that need to be made.

When you throw away a paper plate, it takes almost 5 years for it to break down! That paper plate just sits in a trash pile that gets bigger and bigger. Imagine if every family in America used paper plates! That would be one massive pile of trash! Instead of using paper plates, plastic cups, and paper towels that you'll just throw away, use dishes and towels that you can use over and over again.

Shop Differently

What do you do with all those plastic grocery bags after you use them? Most people just throw them away. However, plastic is not a natural material so it can't break down easily. Instead, it just sits in a pile of trash forever. This is why cities all over the world are making an effort to ban plastic bags. Instead, bring a tote bag or backpack with you to the grocery store to carry your groceries. Or buy fabric or mesh shopping bags you can use over and over again.

Take Action Every Day!

The Earth gives us so many wonderful gifts. It gives us food and water to survive, it offers us days full of sunshine for comfort, and it provides breathtaking nature for us to enjoy. The Earth takes care of us, so we need to take care of the Earth. Never question the power you have to help our planet stay healthy. Make little changes every day and you just might see big changes happen right before your eyes!

1   Which statement best describes the main message of the first paragraph?

Ⓐ   People should think about their actions.

Ⓑ   People should spend more time outdoors.

Ⓒ   People should appreciate the planet more.

Ⓓ   People should live healthier lives.

2   The author states that looking after the Earth "is all about balance." Which sentences from the section titled "Choose Your Appliances Wisely" best support this statement?

Ⓐ   *We have all become used to appliances. Washing machines, microwave ovens, and even robotic vacuum cleaners all make our lives easier.*

Ⓑ   *You don't have to give these things up to help the Earth. You just have to think carefully about which ones to buy.*

Ⓒ   *New machines are built with saving energy in mind. If you have really old appliances, think about replacing them with new ones.*

Ⓓ   *When you do buy appliances, they come with energy ratings. These tell you how efficient the items are.*

3   Use details from the passage to complete the web below.

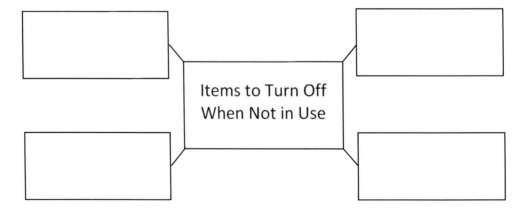

Items to Turn Off When Not in Use

4   Paragraph 5 describes problems and solutions. Which sentence from the paragraph describes a solution?

    Ⓐ   *It's also important to know that many things will keep using electricity even when they're turned off.*

    Ⓑ   *Televisions, computers, and phone chargers can stay in standby mode and keep using electricity when there's no good reason to.*

    Ⓒ   *This can easily be prevented by turning the items off at the wall.*

    Ⓓ   *It's an easy habit to get into and you won't even notice the difference.*

5   Complete the web below by listing **three** ways to stay cool without using electricity.

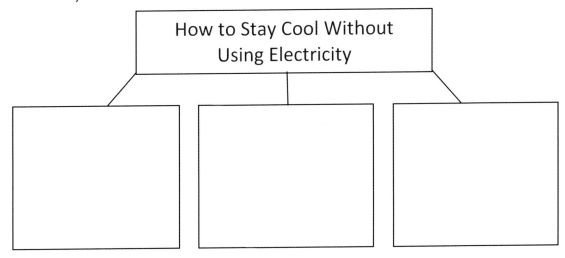

How to Stay Cool Without Using Electricity

6   What does the art in the section titled "Recycle and Reuse" most help readers understand?

    Ⓐ   what types of items can be recycled

    Ⓑ   how to recycle household goods

    Ⓒ   what happens to recycled items

    Ⓓ   how long it takes to recycle items

7 Read this sentence from the passage.

It gives us food and water to survive, it offers us days full of sunshine for comfort, and it provides breathtaking nature for us to enjoy.

What does the word *breathtaking* mean?

Ⓐ   delicate

Ⓑ   rare

Ⓒ   shocking

Ⓓ   stunning

8 Which statement describes a main theme of the passage? Select **one** box to show the statement most related to the passage.

☐   Practice makes perfect.

☐   A picture is worth a thousand words.

☐   Honesty is the best policy.

☐   Everyone can make a difference.

☐   Good things come to those who wait.

☐   Actions speak louder than words.

9 What does the art at the beginning of the passage represent? Explain how it relates to the main idea of the passage.

_____

_____

_____

_____

_____

10 Complete the table below by listing the main bad habit people have for each item and what people should do to avoid wasting electricity.

How Bad Habits Waste Electricity

Item	What People Do	What People Should Do
television		
computer		

11 List **two** benefits of using a fan instead of an air conditioner.

1: _____

_____

2: _____

_____

12 How does the Energy Star program make shopping smart easy? Use **two** details from the passage to support your answer.

_____

_____

_____

_____

_____

13 The author describes how human activity "causes trash to build up in landfills." Use details from the section "Recycle and Reuse" to describe **two** ways that people can reduce trash.

1: _____

_____

2: _____

_____

14 What change does the author suggest that people make in the section titled "Shop Differently"? Do you think this would be an easy change for people to make?

_____

_____

_____

_____

_____

15   The author states that protecting the planet is all about balance. Describe **three** examples from the passage where people have to balance what they want with doing the right thing for the environment.

_____

_____

_____

_____

_____

_____

_____

_____

_____

_____

_____

_____

_____

_____

_____

_____

_____

Practice Set 8

Opinion Piece

Save the Park

Instructions

This set has one passage for you to read. The passage is followed by questions.

Read each question carefully. For each multiple choice question, fill in the circle for the correct answer. For other types of questions, follow the instructions given. Some of the questions require a written answer. Write your answer on the lines provided.

Save the Park

Dear Mayor Boscov,

My name is Annie White and I am a student at Perkins Elementary School. I want to ask for your help to clean up our town's park and river. A few years ago, I walked to the park with my mother almost every day. It was a beautiful place to be, but now it is full of trash and graffiti. Our river is full of plastic bags, bottles, and other trash. I would still like to go to the park but it is no longer inviting at all.

I know that if we get all the students in my school to work together we can make the park a safe and fun place for everyone again. First, I talked to my friends in grade 4. Second, I talked to my teacher to ask if we can get the whole class to help. My teacher, Ms. Gonzales, said that we have to ask you, the Mayor, for help and your permission to clean up the park. As a part of our English class, she said we can choose to write you a letter about cleaning up the park. Ms. Gonzales is excited about grade 4 wanting to help clean the park. She has even agreed to be the project manager to help organize everybody that offers to help.

Grade 4 wants to help, and my brother's class will help too. He is in grade 6. Maybe we can get the whole school to help. I hope that you will give us permission to clean the park and give us some help. We need some adults to help us with the project and help us raise money. I know that we cannot do it by ourselves, but if the school works together we can quickly cut back all the overgrown grass, plant new gardens, take away the trash, fix the broken fountain, repaint the benches, and clean the river. We could even add a new children's playground or exercise equipment to suit all ages.

I also would like to paint a mural on the wall behind the fountain. If we want the park to be beautiful we must help each other and do it together. I am the best at painting in my art class, and I asked my art teacher, Mr. Sanchez, if he could help us make a design for the wall. Mr. Sanchez said that if grades 4 and 6 will help clean the park, he will help us design the mural.

I know that fixing and cleaning the park and the river also needs money. The park will benefit everyone in the community, so it makes sense to raise money from the people in the community. My idea is to put an article about fixing the park in the local newspaper. We can write about how much we want to fix the park and clean the river. We can write about all the problems. We can also write about how great the park could be. We can ask for everyone's help and request donations. We can also put up posters on town noticeboards. Also, everybody goes to the town center. We can give out flyers at the town center.

Miss Williams is teaching our social studies class about government and how big changes happen. She is also teaching us about how small changes can happen and how people can come together to create change. Miss Williams will help us with this project. She will help us make the posters and flyers to give out. She said it will be a great learning experience for us to be part of a real-life example of creating change.

Lastly, I know that we need help to clean the river. I think we need your help to clean the river because it would be dangerous for students to go in the river to clean the trash. Can you please organize a safe way to clean the river?

I hope that you will help us by giving us permission to clean the park. I hope that you can also help us raise money, and ask for adults in your office to help us work on the project. My teachers, classmates, and my parents are all excited about the idea and want to help. All we need to get started is your support.

Thank you for reading my letter.

Sincerely,

Annie White

We can make the park a lovely place that people want to be!

1 In which sentence from the first paragraph does Annie state the main purpose of the letter? Tick the box for the **one** best answer.

☐ My name is Annie White and I am a student at Perkins Elementary School.

☐ I want to ask for your help to clean up our town's park and river.

☐ A few years ago, I walked to the park with my mother almost every day.

☐ It was a beautiful place to be, but now it is full of trash and graffiti.

☐ Our river is full of plastic bags, bottles, and other trash.

☐ I would still like to go to the park but it is no longer inviting at all.

2 Read this sentence from the passage.

I know that if we get all the students in my school to work together we can make the park a safe and fun place for everyone again.

Which word best describes the tone of the sentence?

Ⓐ annoyed

Ⓑ hopeful

Ⓒ saddened

Ⓓ uncertain

3 A theme of the third paragraph is the importance of –

Ⓐ communication

Ⓑ family

Ⓒ fitness

Ⓓ teamwork

4   According to the passage, what does Annie personally want to do to improve the park?

     Ⓐ   plant new gardens

     Ⓑ   repaint the benches

     Ⓒ   paint a mural

     Ⓓ   remove the trash

5   Complete the web below by listing **three** ways that Annie wants to let the people of the town know about the issue and ask for help and donations.

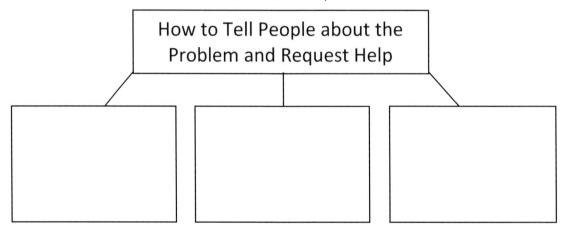

6   One of the tasks to be done is to fix the broken fountain. Which word means about the same as *fix*?

     Ⓐ   rebuild

     Ⓑ   remove

     Ⓒ   repair

     Ⓓ   replace

7   Complete the table below by listing **two** more teachers Annie has spoken to and what each teacher has agreed to do.

Teacher	Help Offered
Ms. Gonzales	be the project manager and organize all the volunteers

8   What is the main purpose of the letter overall?

   Ⓐ   to show the importance of the park to the community

   Ⓑ   to request funding from the mayor to fix the park

   Ⓒ   to ask for the mayor's support to clean up the park

   Ⓓ   to make the mayor feel bad about the state of the park

9   According to the first paragraph, how has the state of the park affected Annie personally? Use **two** details from the passage in your answer.

_____

_____

_____

_____

_____

10   Look at the photograph next to the first paragraph. How do you think this photograph would make readers feel? Do you think this would encourage them to want to clean up the park? Explain your answer.

_____

_____

_____

_____

_____

11   Annie wants to fix problems with the park and add new things to the park. List **three** new things Annie suggests adding to the park.

1: _____

2: _____

3: _____

12   Describe **two** details Annie gives to show that Ms. Gonzales supports the project.

1: _____

_____

2: _____

_____

13   Why does Annie want to put an article about fixing the park in the local newspaper? Use **two** details from the passage to support your answer.

_____

_____

_____

_____

_____

14   Look at the photograph at the end of the passage. How does the photograph create hope? Explain your answer.

_____

_____

_____

_____

_____

15   In the letter, Annie states that she knows "we cannot do it by ourselves." How is Annie encouraging others to help? Describe **three** ways that Annie is getting other people involved in the project.

_____

_____

_____

_____

_____

_____

_____

_____

_____

_____

_____

_____

_____

_____

_____

Practice Set 9

Interview

Interview with Valarie Smyth, Former Peace Corps Volunteer

Instructions

This set has one passage for you to read. The passage is followed by questions.

Read each question carefully. For each multiple choice question, fill in the circle for the correct answer. For other types of questions, follow the instructions given. Some of the questions require a written answer. Write your answer on the lines provided.

Interview with Valarie Smyth, Former Peace Corps Volunteer

Can you please introduce yourself?

Sure! My name is Valarie and I'm from California. I live in San Diego with my dog, Pickles. I studied education in college and I am proud to have been a Peace Corps volunteer.

What is the Peace Corps?

The Peace Corps is an American organization that sends volunteers all over the world to help less fortunate people and communities fight hunger, protect the planet, improve education, and more. This organization was created by President John F. Kennedy back in 1961 and has since sent volunteers to over 140 countries.

Why did you become a Peace Corps volunteer?

Well, it all started with a dream to help others. When I was in middle school, I started volunteering at an orphanage in Mexico during the summer. I would teach the children how to speak English and help to build playgrounds. It felt really great to give back and I loved learning about new cultures. So, when I discovered that the Peace Corps would send me to another country to help others and learn about new cultures for free, I just knew that this was something I needed to do!

How does someone become a Peace Corps Volunteer?

First, you need to have a big heart that is ready to help. Then, you need to go to college to get a good education. You can study medicine, science, wildlife, art, or something else that you love. I applied to join after doing two years of a teaching degree. You should also start volunteering at a soup kitchen, afterschool club, a community organization, or any charity that you care about. It doesn't matter what you choose to do – it just matters that you learn a skill that you can share and that you show that you love to volunteer. Then, you can apply for the Peace Corps!

Where did you go and what did you do?

I was sent to Bulgaria to teach English! I worked in a school that didn't have a lot of money for books or even many teachers. It was my job to come up with creative ways to learn such as with games, songs, and clubs. I also started volunteering in a home for children whose parents were too sick or poor to care for them. I studied the Bulgarian language every day, which helped me create friendships in the community. My days were very busy with teaching English, working in the children's home, and learning Bulgarian. However, I loved every minute of it.

How long were you there?

I was in Bulgaria for 27 months. This is the standard amount of time that each volunteer is placed in a Peace Corps country. The first 3 months were for training, and the remaining 24 months were carrying out my volunteering role.

Will every volunteer go to Bulgaria?

No, not every volunteer will go to Bulgaria. In fact, the Peace Corps sends volunteers to over 140 countries around the world. Some volunteers may go to Colombia to build bridges. Some volunteers may go to Uganda to work with sick children in hospitals. Some volunteers may go to Thailand to start a sports team for young kids. It all depends on what each volunteer is good at doing or what they have studied in university.

You lived abroad for a long time. What did you miss most from home?

That's an easy question! The thing that I missed most from home was American food! Hamburgers, French fries, Dr. Pepper, and cheese! I would even dream about food! Bulgarian food was very delicious, but sometimes I just wanted a taste of comfort food from home! Of course, I also missed my family and my friends, but I made lots of new friends in Bulgaria.

What did you do after you finished your job in the Peace Corps?

First, I took some time to travel around Europe. I visited the beaches of Greece, ate lots of yummy food in Turkey, and then headed to Italy to visit historic cathedrals and see classic works of art. Once I returned home, I spent some time visiting with my family and friends. Eventually, I went back to school to finish my teaching degree. Now I am a middle school teacher and I love waking up every morning to work with some amazing kids.

Would you recommend being a Peace Corps volunteer to others?

Absolutely! The Peace Corps offers Americans of all ages, genders, and backgrounds a unique opportunity to see the world while making a difference in the lives and communities of others. Volunteers learn new skills and languages, make lifelong friends, and have amazing stories to tell for the rest of their lives! People have lots of respect for Peace Corps volunteers and it's something that every volunteer can be proud of.

Thank you very much for interviewing with me today. Is there anything else you'd like to tell our readers?

Yes, I'd like to tell your readers that education is something that can be shared! If you have a great teacher, go to a great school and are able to read this, then you are already so powerful! Take what you learn and share it with the world. You can make a difference!

1   Which detail about Valarie from her first answer is most important to the rest of the interview?

    Ⓐ   She is from San Diego, California.

    Ⓑ   She has a dog named Pickles.

    Ⓒ   She studied education in college.

    Ⓓ   She has been a Peace Corps volunteer.

2   Answer the questions below to summarize facts given about the Peace Corps.

Who was the Peace Corps created by? _____

When was the Peace Corps created? _____

How many countries have Peace Corps volunteers been to? _____

3   Based on her answer to "Where did you go and what did you do?", which word would Valarie most likely use to describe her time in the Peace Corps?

    Ⓐ   stressful

    Ⓑ   tiring

    Ⓒ   lonely

    Ⓓ   rewarding

4   In the answer to "Will every volunteer go to Bulgaria?", Valarie gives examples of what volunteers have done in different locations. Complete the table by summarizing the examples given.

Country	Volunteer Work

5   What does the information in the answer to "Will every volunteer go to Bulgaria?" suggest about how each volunteer will be assigned a country?

Ⓐ   by which country the volunteer would most like to visit

Ⓑ   by which country has needs that match the volunteer's skills

Ⓒ   by which country is most seriously in need of help

Ⓓ   by which country has a language the volunteer can speak

6   How is the information in the answer to "What did you do after you finished your job in the Peace Corps?" organized?

Ⓐ   cause and effect

Ⓑ   chronological order

Ⓒ   problem and solution

Ⓓ   fact and opinion

7 What is Valarie mainly trying to do in her answer to the last question?

Ⓐ   inform people

Ⓑ   inspire people

Ⓒ   entertain people

Ⓓ   warn people

8 Read this sentence from the interview.

First, you need to have a big heart that is ready to help.

The phrase "a big heart" means that you have to be –

Ⓐ   creative

Ⓑ   fit

Ⓒ   generous

Ⓓ   talented

9 Read Valarie's answer to "Why did you become a Peace Corps volunteer?" Describe **two** reasons she enjoyed volunteering at the orphanage in Mexico.

1: _____

_____

2: _____

_____

10 Based on your answer to Question 9, describe how Valarie's experience volunteering in Mexico encouraged her to join the Peace Corps.

_____

_____

_____

_____

_____

11 Before becoming a Peace Corps volunteer, Valarie describes how people need to get an education. Do people need to study a certain area to get accepted into the Peace Corps? Explain your answer.

_____

_____

_____

_____

_____

12 Valarie describes how the Peace Corps sent her to Bulgaria to teach English. List **two** details from her background that help explain why she was given this role.

1: _____

_____

2: _____

_____

13   In the interview, Valarie is asked what she missed most from home. Is this question important to the main idea of the interview? Explain why or why not.

_____

_____

_____

_____

_____

14   The second last question asks if Valarie would recommend being a Peace Corps volunteer to others. Use Valarie's answer to summarize **three** benefits of being a Peace Corps volunteer.

```
        ┌─────────────────────────────┐
        │   Benefits of Being a Peace │
        │      Corps Volunteer        │
        └─────────────────────────────┘
   ┌──────────┐   ┌──────────┐   ┌──────────┐
   │          │   │          │   │          │
   │          │   │          │   │          │
   │          │   │          │   │          │
   └──────────┘   └──────────┘   └──────────┘
```

15 Being a Peace Corps volunteer would be rewarding, but it would also be challenging. Describe **three** ways being a Peace Corps volunteer would be challenging. Use details from the passage to support your answer.

_____

_____

_____

_____

_____

_____

_____

_____

_____

_____

_____

_____

_____

_____

_____

_____

Practice Set 10

History Article

The First Olympic Games – They Sure Have Changed!

Instructions

This set has one passage for you to read. The passage is followed by questions.

Read each question carefully. For each multiple choice question, fill in the circle for the correct answer. For other types of questions, follow the instructions given. Some of the questions require a written answer. Write your answer on the lines provided.

The First Olympic Games – They Sure Have Changed!

The first Olympics began in the city of Olympia, Greece, about 3,000 years ago. That is how the event got the name "Olympics." The Olympics were held to honor the god, Zeus. The Greek people liked sports and competitions. So the Olympics were very popular.

Now, the Olympic competition is split into the Summer Olympics and the Winter Olympics. Each Olympics is held in a different city. They are held every other two years.

There are many more sports in today's Olympics than the first Games. The events in the first Olympics were only made up of running races. Boxing and wrestling matches were soon added. Discus and javelin throwing and chariot races were added after that.

During the first Olympics, nearly all of the Greek cities sent teams to compete. If some of the cities were at war with each other, the wars were put on hold for the Games. Athletes from these cities were then sent to compete peacefully. Today's Olympics have athletes from over 200 countries! Again, the purpose is to compete peacefully. It is also to celebrate equality, acceptance, and cooperation around the world.

Only men could compete in the first Games. Married women were not allowed to compete or even watch the events. Eventually, women were allowed to attend the events. Beginning in the Paris Olympics of 1900, women could participate.

The symbol for the Olympic Games is five connecting rings. Each ring is a different color: blue, yellow, black, green, and red. The rings stand for the continents that compete: North and South America, Asia, Africa, Europe, and Australia. The way the rings connect represents how the Olympics brings the whole world together.

The winners in the first Olympics won a crown made of leaves to wear on their heads. When the winners went home to their city-states, they were treated like superstars. Today's winners receive medals and flowers. There are three medals given in each competition. Gold is for first place, silver is for second place, and bronze is given for third place. The winners are treated like hometown heroes when they go home, too. Some countries may give money and gifts to the medal winners.

Running was a sport in the first Olympics and is still a sport in today's Olympics.

There is an Olympic Torch that is lit in Olympia, Greece, several months before the opening ceremony. The torch travels around Greece by a short relay. Different people run so far and hand off the torch to a new runner. Then this runner runs and then gives the torch to another runner. This continues as the torch travels around the world. It ends up in the host country's stadium on the opening day of the Games. The final runner runs toward the cauldron and uses the torch to start the flame in the stadium. After the flame is lit, it burns throughout the Games.

The Opening Ceremony begins the Olympics. The country that is hosting the Olympics plans the ceremony. An important part of the Opening Ceremony is the Parade of Nations. This is when all the athletes march into the stadium. They come into the stadium, country by country. The countries march by alphabetical order. They wear their countries' colors and carry the flag. They also carry the name of the country on a banner. It is a great honor for each person to represent their country.

After the athletes have entered the stadium, different Olympic Committee Presidents give speeches. They then ask the leader of the host country, state, or city to declare that the Games are "open." Then the host country's flag is raised and the national song is sung. There is more music, singing, dance, and theater performances from the host country.

At the end of the Olympic Games, the Closing Ceremony is held. One athlete from each country carries a flag from their country into the stadium. The athletes from each country march behind the flag carrier. The Greek flag is first in the march in honor of the first Olympics. The host country's flag ends the march. The other countries march in alphabetical order.

After the parade, a ceremony is held. The Olympic flag is lowered as the anthem is played. The mayor of the host city hands this flag to the International Olympic Committee President. The President hands it to the mayor of the next host city. The flag of that country is then raised. The country's song is sung.

There is a performance to watch. Part of this performance shows the next host city. There may be performers in native costumes or a slide show of pictures of that country. The President gives a speech to thank all of the athletes and volunteers. The Games are "closed." The Olympic flame is blown out. Often there are fireworks. This ends the Games until the next event.

1   According to the passage, where did the name "Olympics" come from?

    Ⓐ   a god

    Ⓑ   a place

    Ⓒ   a person

    Ⓓ   a sport

2   Read these sentences from the passage.

The Greek people liked sports and competitions. So the Olympics were very popular.

Which term best describes how the information in the sentences is organized?

    Ⓐ   fact and opinion

    Ⓑ   problem and solution

    Ⓒ   cause and effect

    Ⓓ   comparison

3   Read this sentence from the passage.

If some of the cities were at war with each other, the wars were put on hold for the Games.

The phrase "put on hold" means that the wars were –

    Ⓐ   ended

    Ⓑ   moved

    Ⓒ   paused

    Ⓓ   solved

4   Complete the table below by selecting the box that best describes when each sport was added.

	First	Next	Last
boxing	☐	☐	☐
chariot races	☐	☐	☐
discus	☐	☐	☐
javelin	☐	☐	☐
running	☐	☐	☐
wrestling	☐	☐	☐

5   Select the **two** sentences from paragraph 8 that best show the meaning of *relay*.

☐   There is an Olympic Torch that is lit in Olympia, Greece, several months before the opening ceremony.

☐   Different people run so far and hand off the torch to a new runner.

☐   Then this runner runs and then gives the torch to another runner.

☐   This continues as the torch travels around the world. It ends up in the host country's stadium on the opening day of the Games.

☐   The final runner runs toward the cauldron and uses the torch to start the flame in the stadium.

☐   After the flame is lit, it burns throughout the Games.

6 Which detail given about the Parade of Nations at the Opening Ceremony is an opinion?

Ⓐ   It involves all the nations marching into the stadium.

Ⓑ   The countries enter and march by alphabetical order.

Ⓒ   The entrants wear the colors of their country.

Ⓓ   It is a great honor to represent one's country in the parade.

7 According to paragraph 4, what is a similarity between the purpose of the first Olympics and the Olympics today? Use **two** details from the paragraph to support your answer.

_____

_____

_____

_____

_____

8 What major change occurred at the Paris Olympics of 1900? Use **two** details from the passage to support your answer.

_____

_____

_____

_____

9   Describe **two** features of the Olympic rings symbol that represent countries of the world coming together.

1: _____

_____

2: _____

_____

10   Compare how winning athletes were honored at the first Olympics and how they are honored today. Describe **one** similarity and **one** difference.

Similarity: _____

_____

Difference: _____

_____

11   What does the photograph on the second page of the passage show? Describe the tradition represented in the photograph.

_____

_____

_____

_____

_____

12   How is the first and last country to march in the Closing Ceremony selected? Use **two** details from the passage to support your answer.

_____

_____

_____

_____

_____

13   Describe **two** ways the Closing Ceremony introduces the host of the next Olympics.

1: _____

_____

2: _____

_____

14   How can you tell that the modern Olympics honors the fact that the Olympics first began in Greece? Use **two** details from the passage to support your answer.

_____

_____

_____

_____

15 Describe **three** ways the Olympics have changed since they were first held in Greece. Use details from the passage to support your answer.

_____

_____

_____

_____

_____

_____

_____

_____

_____

_____

_____

_____

_____

_____

_____

_____

_____

Practice Set 11

Flyers

Set of Three Flyers

Instructions

This set has several passages for you to read. Each passage is followed by questions.

Read each question carefully. For each multiple choice question, fill in the circle for the correct answer. For other types of questions, follow the instructions given. Some of the questions require a written answer. Write your answer on the lines provided.

Bake Sale

Helpers on Hand is a charity group focused on helping those in need. The group raises money by organizing many local events. This year, the volunteers have been busy baking Valentine's Day treats. There will be cakes, cookies, chocolates, sweets, red toffee apples, and so much more. Every good for sale has been made by our volunteers. This means that all the money raised will go straight to those who need it most. Please come along and support our group and help us keep making a difference to those in need.

♥ *Valentine's Day* ♥

BAKE SALE

SAT FEBRUARY 14 from two to six PM | **GREEN STREET TOWN LIBRARY**

Proceeds to benefit HELPERS ON HAND

EAT YOUR **HEART OUT** AND BENEFIT those in need

FREE GIFT WRAPPING! FREE GIFT CARD TO ADD YOUR SPECIAL MESSAGE TO!

1 Which sentence from the first paragraph supports the idea that there will be a wide variety of baked goods?

   Ⓐ   *This year, the volunteers have been busy baking Valentine's Day treats.*

   Ⓑ   *There will be cakes, cookies, chocolates, sweets, red toffee apples, and so much more.*

   Ⓒ   *Every good for sale has been made by our volunteers.*

   Ⓓ   *This means that all the money raised will go straight to those who need it most.*

2 As it is used in the flyer, what does the word *benefit* mean?

   Ⓐ   assist

   Ⓑ   educate

   Ⓒ   employ

   Ⓓ   feed

3 Complete the table below to give the details of the bake sale.

Valentine's Day Bake Sale

Day	
Date	
Time	
Location	

4   The passage emphasizes that the goods have all been baked by volunteers. Why is this detail most important?

      Ⓐ   It shows that every dollar that people spend will go to the charity.

      Ⓑ   It suggests that the baked goods will be fresh.

      Ⓒ   It explains how every item has been made with love.

      Ⓓ   It tells why charities need many volunteers.

5   How does the style of the text for "Bake Sale" on the flyer suit the content of the flyer? Explain your answer.

_____

_____

_____

_____

_____

6   How does the passage and flyer suggest that the goods purchased would make suitable Valentine's Day gifts? Use **two** details from the passage or flyer to support your answer.

_____

_____

_____

_____

_____

Summer Art Workshop

Jolie's parents suggested she find a fun activity to do during her summer vacation. Jolie loves art and found an art workshop held nearby. She found this flyer giving details about the workshop.

All materials provided! Qualified and experienced staff on hand to help! You bring yourself and comfortable clothes. We'll take care of the rest!

CALL NOW TO BOOK YOUR SPOT! PLACES FILLING FAST!

1   Read these sentences from the flyer.

> **All materials provided! Qualified and experienced staff on hand to help! You bring yourself and comfortable clothes. We'll take care of the rest!**

These sentences mainly make attending the workshop seem –

Ⓐ   trouble-free and easy

Ⓑ   educational and informative

Ⓒ   fun and exciting

Ⓓ   challenging and inspiring

2   Based on the details in the flyer, what does the summer art workshop provide?

Ⓐ   hats and sunscreen

Ⓑ   aprons and smocks

Ⓒ   food and drinks

Ⓓ   journals and workbooks

3   Complete the diagram below to show **four** types of painting included in the art workshop.

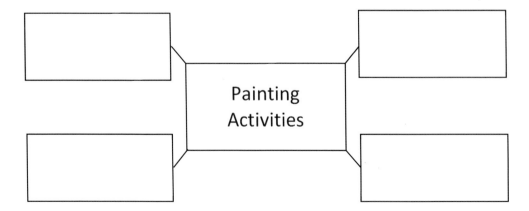

4   Which **two** activities for the 8 to 10 age group are represented in illustrations? Select the **two** correct answers.

☐   Pottery

☐   Cap making

☐   T-shirt painting

☐   Zoo safari

☐   Yoga

5   Does the workshop only include art activities or does it include other types of activities as well? Use **two** details from the flyer to support your answer.

_____

_____

_____

_____

_____

6   Compare the activities for the 13 to 16 age group with those for the 3 to 7 age group. Explain how the activities are different for the 13 to 16 age group.

_____

_____

_____

_____

_____

Josie's Guitar Lessons

Josie has been studying and playing music for most of her life. Born into a musical family, she had experience playing the violin, piano, trumpet, and drums before the age of 10. She developed a love of music and kept playing a range of instruments all through her teenage years. However, it was the guitar that became her true passion. She has enjoyed playing at festivals and events, as well as at weddings and formals. She now wants to share her love of music with others and inspire young people to take the time to develop their musical talent. Josie now runs guitar lessons and classes at her home music studio. Josie made the flyer below to promote her business.

1   As it is used in the flyer, what does the word *jam* mean?

   Ⓐ   to press something tightly between two surfaces

   Ⓑ   to block something by crowding it

   Ⓒ   to fill something too tightly

   Ⓓ   to play music together

2   Based on the flyer, how would someone register for guitar lessons?

   Ⓐ   send an email

   Ⓑ   call the phone number

   Ⓒ   sign up on the website

   Ⓓ   visit Josie's home studio

3   What is the main benefit implied of the group classes over the standard guitar lessons?

   Ⓐ   The group classes are better suited to beginners.

   Ⓑ   The group classes have a lower cost per hour.

   Ⓒ   The group classes make it easier to learn.

   Ⓓ   The group classes are available more often.

4   Which detail from the flyer supports the idea that there is no risk for new students considering starting guitar lessons?

   Ⓐ   The first lesson is free.

   Ⓑ   The classes suit all ages.

   Ⓒ   There are classes for all levels.

   Ⓓ   The cost is $25 per hour.

5   How is the cost of the lessons presented in a clever way on the flyer? Explain your answer.

_____

_____

_____

_____

6   Which detail from the side section about group classes supports the idea that Josie's classes suit students with different amounts of experience?

_____

_____

_____

_____

7   How do the details given about Josie's childhood help explain why she started her business? Use **two** details from the passage in your answer.

_____

_____

_____

_____

_____

_____

Practice Set 12

Advertisements

Set of Three Advertisements

Instructions

This set has several passages for you to read. Each passage is followed by questions.

Read each question carefully. For each multiple choice question, fill in the circle for the correct answer. For other types of questions, follow the instructions given. Some of the questions require a written answer. Write your answer on the lines provided.

Belgian Waffles

Belgian waffles are a popular choice for breakfast, brunch, or as a dessert. They are sort of like thick pancakes, but they're made to have a crunchy outside and a soft inside. Think of them as being like a doughnut, but with a crunchier outside. Belgian waffles are wonderfully versatile. They can be topped with fresh fruit and cream, bacon and eggs, grilled banana, caramel fudge and ice cream, or any other savory or sweet combination you choose.

You can make Belgian waffles yourself, but you need a special waffle maker to get the crisscross pattern and the right texture. Unless you are making waffles all the time, it's probably not worth the expense to have a special machine just for that! An easier option is to buy waffles ready to go. You simply heat them in a regular toaster or in an oven, add your chosen topping, and enjoy!

1   Which serving idea given in the passage is shown on the advertisement?

     Ⓐ   fresh fruit and cream

     Ⓑ   bacon and eggs

     Ⓒ   grilled banana

     Ⓓ   caramel fudge and ice cream

2   Which word or phrase from the advertisement tells the texture of the waffles?

     Ⓐ   Just Heat and Eat!

     Ⓑ   Simply delicious!

     Ⓒ   Yummy

     Ⓓ   Light & Crispy

3   The advertisement includes the statement, "Just Heat and Eat!" Which idea from the passage does this statement mainly support?

     ☐   *Belgian waffles are a popular choice for breakfast, brunch, or as a dessert.*

     ☐   *They are sort of like thick pancakes, but they're made to have a crunchy outside and a soft inside.*

     ☐   *Belgian waffles are wonderfully versatile.*

     ☐   *You can make Belgian waffles yourself, but you need a special waffle maker to get the crisscross pattern and the right texture.*

     ☐   *Unless you are making waffles all the time, it's probably not worth the expense to have a special machine just for that!*

     ☐   *An easier option is to buy waffles ready to go.*

4 How are Belgian waffles versatile? Describe **two** ways they are versatile.

1: _____

_____

2: _____

_____

5 What two products does the author compare Belgian waffles to in the first paragraph? Explain why the author makes these comparisons.

_____

_____

_____

_____

_____

6 How does the way the advertisement is presented make Belgian waffles seem like a fun thing to eat? Use **two** details from the advertisement to support your answer.

_____

_____

_____

_____

Silicone Teething Beads

Lindy's mother has a business making silicone teething beads. When babies are teething, their new teeth are trying to break through from the gums. The teeth push against the gums. This can cause the baby to be grumpy and upset. Babies often feel better when they have something to chew on. A soft item to chew on can reduce discomfort.

Lindy's mother makes silicone teething beads for this purpose. The parent can wear a necklace or bracelet of beads. This makes it easy for the parent to have something safe for the baby to chew on ready and waiting whenever it is needed.

1   Read this sentence from the passage.

A soft item to chew on can reduce discomfort.

As it is used in the sentence, which word means about the same as *discomfort*?

Ⓐ   boredom

Ⓑ   hunger

Ⓒ   pain

Ⓓ   worry

2   Based on the first two paragraphs, which statement describes the main purpose of the teething beads?

Ⓐ   They help a baby's teeth come through faster.

Ⓑ   They reduce how upset a baby feels when teething.

Ⓒ   They ensure that new teeth are strong and healthy.

Ⓓ   They prevent babies from chewing on unsuitable items.

3   Which **two** words from the advertisement describe the texture of the silicone beads?

☐   soft

☐   chewy

☐   non-toxic

☐   easy

☐   safe

4   Describe **two** details in the illustration of the baby that support the main ideas.

1: _____

_____

2: _____

_____

5   The advertisement states that the products do not contain the chemicals BPA, PVC, phthalates, cadmium, and lead. Why would it be important that the products do not contain these chemicals? Explain your answer.

_____

_____

_____

_____

_____

6   Does the style of the advertisement suit the product being advertised? Explain why you feel that way.

_____

_____

_____

_____

_____

Bathroom Cleaner

While looking through a magazine, Miss Hayden saw this advertisement for a bathroom cleaner. After reading the advertisement, Miss Hayden was impressed enough to want to purchase the product to see if it would work as well as it claimed.

OUR PROMISE TO YOU
ABSOLUTELY NO SCRUBBING NEEDED! JUST SPRAY AND WIPE FOR SPARKLING RESULTS. OUR PRODUCT DOES ALL THE HARD WORK!

1   What do the three images shown in circles on the advertisement represent?

    Ⓐ   how to use the product

    Ⓑ   the main benefits of the product

    Ⓒ   where the product can be used

    Ⓓ   how fast the product works

2   The advertisement states that the bathroom cleaner "kills 99.9% of viruses and bacteria." Which feature of the product listed does this detail best support?

    Ⓐ   Removes Odors

    Ⓑ   Fights Germs

    Ⓒ   Beats Tough Stains

    Ⓓ   Cuts Through Water Scale

3   The sink shown in the advertisement appears to be sparkling or shimmering. This is most likely used to show that it is –

    Ⓐ   clean

    Ⓑ   new

    Ⓒ   expensive

    Ⓓ   scented

4   Describe **two** ways the information at the bottom of the advertisement shows that the product makes cleaning easy.

     1. _____

     _____

     2. _____

     _____

5   Look at the art of the bubbles shown in the advertisement. What do you think these bubbles represent? Use details from the advertisement in your answer.

_____

_____

_____

_____

_____

6   Which feature shown in the advertisement would most help Miss Hayden find the product in a grocery store? Explain your answer.

_____

_____

_____

_____

_____

Practice Set 13

Science Article

Amazing Inventions in Our Homes

Instructions

This set has one passage for you to read. The passage is followed by questions.

Read each question carefully. For each multiple choice question, fill in the circle for the correct answer. For other types of questions, follow the instructions given. Some of the questions require a written answer. Write your answer on the lines provided.

Amazing Inventions in Our Homes

The New World of 3D Printing

A 3D printer is a device that is able to print out objects. Normal printers you are used to print out images on paper. A 3D printer is able to print out a solid object.

In a few years, you might have a 3D printer at your house. Maybe you won't even go to the store anymore. You might buy a toy design and just print it off yourself! There are 3D printed dresses, pants, and shoes that fit perfectly. There are 3D printed clocks, doorknobs, wheelchairs, and car parts. Some people are 3D printing their houses. Even food has been 3D printed. Would you eat 3D printed chocolate or pizza?

An American man called Charles Hull invented 3D printing. He was a scientist and liked solving problems. In 1983, he was trying to work out how to make tabletops harder. He was using ultraviolet light and he started thinking. *What if I built something layer by layer? Could I harden it using ultraviolet light?* He started to experiment. He was able to make 3D objects of any shape. It was the first 3D printer!

There are lots of different types of 3D printers now. New ones are being tested and invented all the time. Experts think that lots of people will have 3D printers at home soon. You can buy a 3D printer for your home now, but they are still quite costly.

The Rise of Computers

When computers were first invented hardly anyone thought they would end up in peoples' homes. Computers were so huge that they filled a whole room. Why would anyone want that in their house? They were expensive and could only do math problems. You couldn't play games on them or even use the Internet. There was no Internet!

Charles Hull invented 3D printers, and another Charles, Charles Babbage, invented the first computer. Charles Babbage was born over 140 years earlier than Charles Hull.

When he was only eight years old, Charles Babbage went to a unique shop with his mother. "Merlin's Mechanical Museum" was a shop in London full of incredible machines. Mr. Merlin, the shop owner, kept his most special machines up in the attic. He invited Charles and his mother to see them. In the attic was a beautiful automated dancer. She could move just like a human dancer. Charles Babbage was fascinated by her.

After visiting Merlin's shop, Charles became interested in automation. Automation refers to using machines to do things without humans. Charles also loved math. He started wondering how he could use automation in math.

When he grew up, he became a mathematician and invented what he called a difference engine. The difference engine could work out math problems, like adding and subtracting. Charles designed all the plans for his machine, but he never made one. He decided that the difference engine was too simple. He wanted something that could do more by itself. So Charles invented what he called the analytical engine. The analytical engine was the first computer. It had the same main parts as modern computers.

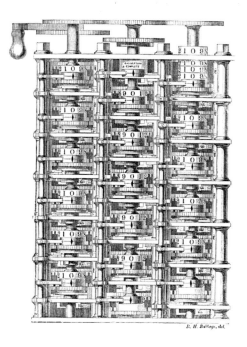

Before this machine was invented, computers were just people who added and subtracted numbers. They wrote the numbers down in tables for other people to use. Humans were the first real computers!

About 100 years later Alan Turing, another British mathematician, created modern computing. Alan always loved science and math, even as a young boy. He found school too easy and started studying science on his own. In 1936, he invented what he named a universal machine. Like Charles Babbage, he designed all the plans but didn't build his machine. Ten years later, he turned his plans into an electronic computer. It was the first modern computer. He carried on inventing. In World War II, Alan Turing invented a code-breaking machine called the Turing machine.

Another important person in early computer invention was Grace Hopper. Grace was a computer programmer. She worked on one of the very first computers. Her job was inventing computer languages.

Grace Hopper was born in New York, in 1906. Grace's mother loved math and taught her daughters to love it too. Grace's parents wanted their girls to have a good education. They encouraged Grace to study hard.

Even as a little girl, Grace loved machines. When she was seven she took an alarm clock apart to see how it worked. The only problem was she couldn't get it back together again! She took apart another seven clocks in their house. Then her mother found out and stopped her.

Grace studied math and physics at college, and did very well. She did so well that she ended up being a teacher at the college. When World War II started, Grace wanted to join the Army. She was told she had to stay and teach. Grace tried to join the Navy instead. Finally, they said she could.

During the war, Harvard University built the Mark 1 computer. It was one of the first computers. Grace was the third person to program it. The Mark 1 was so huge that it filled a big room. It was over 50 feet long and weighed 5 ton!

The Mark 1 took 3 to 6 seconds to add up two numbers. It was really just a massive, slow calculator. You wouldn't want to carry it around in your school bag! No wonder people thought nobody would want computers in their homes. What do you think the early inventors would have thought of our tiny computers? Do you think they would be surprised?

Looking Ahead

It once seemed crazy that computers would be in every home, but it now seems completely normal. It might be just the same for 3D printers. They might become so common that you'll have several of them.

Imagine getting home from school and going to the kitchen. You print out a bowl and a spoon. Then you print out an entire meal to put in your bowl! That might be just what everyday life will be like in the future!

Computers were once so large they took up entire rooms.
Today, things are very different.

1   Read these sentences from the passage.

> **Maybe you won't even go to the store anymore. You might buy a toy design and just print it off yourself!**

Which term best describes these sentences?

Ⓐ   question

Ⓑ   instruction

Ⓒ   prediction

Ⓓ   summary

2   Which sentence from paragraph 4 best supports the idea that 3D printers will continue to improve?

Ⓐ   *There are lots of different types of 3D printers now.*

Ⓑ   *New ones are being tested and invented all the time.*

Ⓒ   *Experts think that lots of people will have 3D printers at home soon.*

Ⓓ   *You can buy a 3D printer for your home now, but they are still quite costly.*

3   Read this sentence from the passage.

> **"Merlin's Mechanical Museum" was a shop in London full of incredible machines.**

What does the word *incredible* mean?

Ⓐ   amazing

Ⓑ   amusing

Ⓒ   enjoyable

Ⓓ   expensive

4   The passage describes how Grace Hopper took apart clocks as a young girl. What is this detail mainly included to show?

Ⓐ   She was determined.

Ⓑ   She was curious.

Ⓒ   She was patient.

Ⓓ   She was talented.

5   Order the inventions of the machines below from earliest to latest. Write the numbers 1 through 4 on the lines to show the order.

_____   analytical engine

_____   difference engine

_____   Turing machine

_____   universal machine

6   Which question asked by the author is included to get readers to think about how 3D printing might affect their lives?

☐   Would you eat 3D printed chocolate or pizza?

☐   What if I built something layer by layer?

☐   Could I harden it using ultraviolet light?

☐   Why would anyone want that in their house?

☐   What do you think the early inventors would have thought of our tiny computers?

☐   Do you think they would be surprised?

7   Which statement best explains how the passage is similar to a biography?

    Ⓐ   It asks readers to imagine the future.

    Ⓑ   It tells about the history of computers.

    Ⓒ   It describes the life and achievements of people.

    Ⓓ   It compares the present with how things were in the past.

8   Scientists often invent new things to solve problems. Describe how Charles Hull is an example of use. Use **two** details from the passage to support your response.

_____

_____

_____

_____

_____

9   Describe **two** reasons that people did not think computers would be used in the home when they were first invented.

1: _____

_____

2: _____

_____

10 How did "Merlin's Mechanical Museum" influence Charles Babbage? In your answer, describe the role the store played in Babbage's inventions.

_____

_____

_____

_____

_____

11 How was Grace Hopper's role in the development of computing different from the role of Charles Babbage and Alan Turing? Explain your answer.

_____

_____

_____

_____

_____

12 Which subject was studied by Charles Babbage, Alan Turing, and Grace Hopper? What does this suggest about the importance of the subject to computing?

_____

_____

_____

_____

_____

13   Read the information in the section titled "Looking Ahead." Circle the word below that best describes how the author seems to feel about the future of 3D printing. Then explain why you selected that word.

cautious   excited   puzzled   curious

_____

_____

_____

_____

14   How does the photograph at the end of the passage show how technology has changed? Explain your answer.

_____

_____

_____

_____

_____

15 How does the history of computing show that 3D printers may become a normal part of the home one day? Use at least **three** details from the passage to support your response.

_____

_____

_____

_____

_____

_____

_____

_____

_____

_____

_____

_____

_____

_____

_____

_____

Practice Set 14

Biography

Elizabeth Blackwell – First Woman U.S. Doctor

Instructions

This set has one passage for you to read. The passage is followed by questions.

Read each question carefully. For each multiple choice question, fill in the circle for the correct answer. For other types of questions, follow the instructions given. Some of the questions require a written answer. Write your answer on the lines provided.

Elizabeth Blackwell – First Woman U.S. Doctor

"It is not easy to be a pioneer -- but oh, it is exciting! I would not trade one moment, even the worst moment, for all the riches in the world."
– Elizabeth Blackwell

What did Elizabeth Blackwell mean when she said these words? Why did she think she was a pioneer? What could be so exciting?

Early Years of Her Life

Elizabeth Blackwell was born in England on February 3, 1821. Her father owned a sugar factory. The factory took raw sugar and turned it into sugar that you can eat.

There were nine children in Elizabeth's family. She had four brothers and four sisters. The children were taught at home by tutors. Elizabeth loved to read. She would always ask for new books. Elizabeth had a happy childhood.

Living in the United States

A fire burned down Mr. Blackwell's sugar factory. Mr. Blackwell decided to move his family to the United States. Elizabeth was eleven years old. The voyage took seven weeks.

Mr. Blackwell built a new sugar factory. The family lived in New York and New Jersey. This was at a time in U.S. history that slaves worked in factories. Mr. Blackwell was against slavery, so he sold his factory and moved to Ohio to do something else. He decided to grow sugar beets.

However, after moving to Ohio, Mr. Blackwell died. The family did not have a lot of money. Elizabeth, her older sisters, and her mother started a school in their home. Elizabeth taught French. The school made enough money to support the family. Later the school was closed; Elizabeth went to teach in Kentucky.

Idea of Becoming a Doctor

One of Elizabeth's friends was very sick. She told Elizabeth that she really wished there were women doctors. She thought women doctors would be kind and caring. That was when Elizabeth decided that she should be a doctor to help women like her friend.

Unfortunately, medical school cost a lot. It would be about $3,000. Elizabeth saved up all of her money from teaching.

Elizabeth wrote this letter home to her family:

July 1846

Dear Family,

My mind is made up. I want to study medicine. I know it will be hard. But I am prepared to work. I want to care for the sick.

Elizabeth

Studying Medicine

Several doctors helped her study. They lent her books to read. They encouraged her to become a doctor. She tried to get into a college to study. Many colleges did not accept her because she was a woman. A woman had not studied medicine before.

She had to apply to 30 colleges until a college in New York finally accepted her. She began her new life as a student at the age of 26. It was such an important event that the local paper wrote:

In the year 1848, there is a young woman student named Elizabeth Blackwell. She comes to class and takes off her bonnet. She is very confident. The men in the class try to behave around her. They are surprised that a woman can do so well.

In fact, Elizabeth got the highest grades. She became the first woman doctor in the United States.

First Work as a Doctor

Elizabeth worked in London and Paris and got lots of experience. Later she returned to New York City. But no hospital would hire a woman. So she opened up her own doctor's office. However, few patients wanted to be treated by a female, and her business struggled.

One of her sisters became a doctor, too. Together they worked at a clinic for needy women and children. When they got enough money, they built a hospital. People began to respect Elizabeth. They saw the good work her hospital did. The hospital also trained many nurses.

Elizabeth then opened up a medical school for women in New York. There were 15 students in the first class. The school would expand and teach more students each year. Elizabeth was also a mentor to other women who wanted to become doctors. She encouraged, helped, and guided them.

Later Years of Her Life

Elizabeth returned to England and set up another clinic. Her sister stayed in New York to run the medical school. Elizabeth was an instructor at the London School of Medicine for Women. She really loved teaching others about medicine. She liked helping women follow their dreams of becoming doctors.

Elizabeth wrote several books. One book described her work as a doctor. It was titled "Pioneer Work in Opening the Medical Field to Women." She wrote about herself in this autobiography.

Elizabeth Blackwell, a True Pioneer

Elizabeth Blackwell was indeed a pioneer, someone who opens up and explores a new area. For Elizabeth, that area was medicine. She studied medicine when many people felt women should not. Because of her work, more and more women became doctors. In her autobiography, Elizabeth wrote:

> *The path to studying medicine is now open. It is not hard for any man or woman who wish to practice medicine. They need only to want to and to work hard.*

Final Years

In 1910, Elizabeth Blackwell died at her home in England.

Women today are able to study medicine and become doctors without many of the barriers that Elizabeth Blackwell faced. Elizabeth Blackwell helped pave the way for the women of today.

1   Read this sentence from the 1846 letter.

My mind is made up.

What does this sentence mean?

Ⓐ   I am afraid.

Ⓑ   I am certain.

Ⓒ   I am smart.

Ⓓ   I am confused.

2   What does the quote at the beginning of the passage suggest about how Elizabeth Blackwell felt about her life?

Ⓐ   She felt upset that she was not rewarded more.

Ⓑ   She felt excited by what the future might hold for women.

Ⓒ   She felt tired from the struggles she had to face.

Ⓓ   She felt proud of what she achieved.

3   Order the problems that Blackwell faced from earliest to latest. Write the numbers 1 through 4 on the lines to show the order.

_____   She could not get accepted into a medical college.

_____   Her doctor's office struggled to have enough patients.

_____   She did not have enough money to attend medical school.

_____   Hospitals in the United States would not hire a female doctor.

4   The 1846 letter that Elizabeth wrote to her family mainly shows her –

Ⓐ   frustration

Ⓑ   determination

Ⓒ   fear

Ⓓ   kindness

5   Which detail from the section "Studying Medicine" best supports the idea that Blackwell did not give up?

Ⓐ   She applied to 30 colleges.

Ⓑ   She started studying at age 26.

Ⓒ   She got the highest grades.

Ⓓ   She appeared confident to her classmates.

6   Which **two** words would the author most likely use to describe Blackwell?

☐   creative

☐   thoughtful

☐   inspiring

☐   passionate

☐   loyal

☐   honest

7   What is the main lesson that can be learned from Blackwell?

   Ⓐ   Stand up to those who stand in your way.

   Ⓑ   Look after the people around you.

   Ⓒ   Take action to achieve your dreams.

   Ⓓ   Put your friends and family first.

8   What is the main purpose of the art and caption at the end of the passage?

   Ⓐ   to show the influence of Blackwell's actions on women today

   Ⓑ   to encourage more women to become doctors

   Ⓒ   to describe how female doctors are different to male doctors

   Ⓓ   to suggest that the women of today keep fighting for change

9   What event first made Blackwell want to become a doctor? Use **two** details from the passage to support your answer.

   _____

   _____

   _____

   _____

   _____

   _____

10   In the section "First Work as a Doctor," the passage describes how Blackwell worked in London and Paris. What does this suggest about the difference between Europe and the United States at the time? Explain your answer.

_____

_____

_____

_____

11   What did Blackwell do when hospitals in the United States would not hire her? Use information from the passage in your answer.

_____

_____

_____

12   Based on your answer to Question 11, explain what Blackwell's actions show about her willingness to take action and help herself.

_____

_____

_____

_____

13   Based on the information in the section "First Work as a Doctor**,**" describe **two** ways that Blackwell encouraged other women to become doctors.

1: _____

_____

2: _____

_____

14   At the end of the passage, the author includes part of Blackwell's autobiography. What does the part of the autobiography included summarize?

_____

_____

_____

_____

_____

_____

15　How did Elizabeth Blackwell help open the medical field to women? In your answer, describe **three** ways she helped make becoming a female doctor possible.

_____

_____

_____

_____

_____

_____

_____

_____

_____

_____

_____

_____

_____

_____

_____

Practice Set 15

How-To Article

How to Learn a New Language

Instructions

This set has one passage for you to read. The passage is followed by questions.

Read each question carefully. For each multiple choice question, fill in the circle for the correct answer. For other types of questions, follow the instructions given. Some of the questions require a written answer. Write your answer on the lines provided.

How to Learn a New Language

Some children grow up using more than one language. For others who only know English, learning a new language can seem scary. But, if we know how to go about it, learning a language does not need to be scary at all. This how-to guide offers some suggestions that will help you learn a new language.

Choose a Language

Sometimes it can be hard to know where to begin. The first step is to select a language to learn. This may seem like an obvious step, but it is good to think about what language is well suited to your situation. If you have friends who speak another language, why not learn that one? It would be easy to practice it with them. They will probably also have helpful suggestions for you.

Or maybe you have an interest in a certain country or culture. If you do, then that can be very motivating. You may even have a desire to visit that country one day. Learning that language would be very helpful if you visit, or even decide to live in that country.

Ignore the Myths

Many people say that they "don't have the brain for language." Some say that "you are better off learning when you are a baby. Babies learn more quickly than adults." Once you start learning a language, you'll find that these things aren't true. In my experience, *anyone* can learn a language. When you think about it, babies take around three or four years to get the basics of a language. Most adults can learn a language to fluency in half, or even a quarter of that time.

Choose Learning Resources

Everybody learns in different ways. Often, visual methods work well. Find a good language learning app that uses pictures or buy some flashcards. Find some instructional videos or websites with videos you can watch. You can also learn just by listening to CDs. This will help you learn how to pronounce new words correctly. Another way to learn is by attending language classes. Language classes can be beneficial because it will give you practice using the language to communicate.

Books may also be helpful. They can be good for explaining complex grammar. Phrase books can also be good to carry around with you. Buy a good dictionary that lists words in your new language and their English definitions. However, be careful with books. Because some books look big, you can quickly feel discouraged and unmotivated.

Start with the Common Words

Spend time learning the most frequently used words first. Often a very small group of words makes up a large percentage of a language. You can find lists of these most common words on the Internet. If you know these words, you can generally communicate your thought. Even if you don't know a specific word, you can explain it using other, more common words. As you progress, you can add more difficult words to your sentences.

Try Shorter More Regular Study Sessions

Instead of sitting down for hours and studying, try lots of smaller study sessions. If you study for long periods of time, you lose concentration quickly. It is also harder to retain the information. Many people prefer shorter study sessions. For example, 10 to 15 minutes a day, every day of the week is good. This would be better than a one- to two-hour session, once a week.

Also, it is better to focus on maybe two or three words a day. If you try to learn more, you will find it hard to remember many of them. You will often confuse yourself and mix up words if you try to learn too many at once.

Practice, Practice, Practice

One of the main things to do when learning a language is to practice it with a native speaker. Allow them to correct you when you make mistakes. Also, listen to the conversations they have with other native speakers. Watch their mouths and listen to how they make the sounds. This will help you with pronunciation.

Don't be Afraid to Make Mistakes

You need to have a good sense of humor when learning a language. If you make a mistake or say the wrong thing, laugh about it. Don't feel embarrassed. If you laugh about your mistakes, you will never forget how to say it correctly. It is much easier to remember funny experiences and stories than a written word on a page. Making mistakes is widely recognized as one of the best ways to learn anything.

Don't Compare Yourself

Sometimes, you may be learning a language with a friend. Or, someone else you know is learning a language at the same time as you are. It is easy to compare your language skills to theirs. It is important that you don't do this. If they are ahead of you, you will only feel downhearted and you may give up. Remember, people learn at different rates.

Measure your Progress in Bigger Blocks

Many language learners look at their progress on a daily or weekly basis. This is generally not a good idea. Because we learn language slowly, comparing our progress from week to week can make us feel as though we are going nowhere. It is better to compare your progress in bigger blocks, such as every six months or after every school term.

Conclusion

Using the tips and tricks above can help you in your quest to learn a new language. Remember to always have fun and enjoy the learning process. Learning a new language can be a very rewarding experience.

1   Based on the first paragraph, what does the author seem to believe about people who only speak one language?

   Ⓐ   They are unsure of which language to try to learn.

   Ⓑ   They think learning a new language will be difficult.

   Ⓒ   They have failed at learning a new language before.

   Ⓓ   They are worried about only being able to speak one language.

2   What is the main purpose of the section titled "Ignore the Myths"?

   Ⓐ   to explain how long it takes to learn a language

   Ⓑ   to suggest that people should start learning a language as young as possible

   Ⓒ   to warn that some people find learning a new language easier than others

   Ⓓ   to stop people believing negative things about learning a language

3   Read this sentence from the passage.

   Language classes can be beneficial because they will give you practice using the language to communicate.

   What does the word *beneficial* mean?

   Ⓐ   challenging

   Ⓑ   friendly

   Ⓒ   helpful

   Ⓓ   inspiring

4 Complete the web below with **four** examples of visual methods that can be used to learn a language.

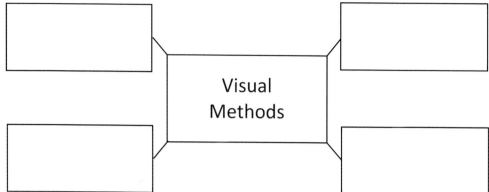

5 In the section titled "Choose Learning Resources," what is the main problem with using books?

  Ⓐ   They do not help you practice speaking a language.

  Ⓑ   They are too heavy to carry around.

  Ⓒ   They can make you feel overwhelmed.

  Ⓓ   They are too serious and take away the fun.

6 The author wants to change the title to one that makes readers feel more excited about learning a language. Select the **two** titles that would best achieve this purpose.

  ☐   Languages of the World

  ☐   Learn a New Language Today!

  ☐   How Many Languages Can You Speak?

  ☐   Let's Learn a New Language! You Can Do It!

  ☐   How I Learned to Speak French

  ☐   New Language Classes Starting Soon

7   Which proverb summarizes a main theme of the section titled "Try Shorter More
Regular Study Sessions"?

Ⓐ   Many hands make light work.

Ⓑ   Slow and steady wins the race.

Ⓒ   Don't judge a book by its cover.

Ⓓ   The early bird gets the worm.

8   Based on your answer to Question 7, describe **two** ways the section relates to the
proverb you selected.

1: _____

_____

2: _____

_____

9   Read this sentence from the section titled "Choose a Language."

If you have friends who speak another language, why not learn that one?

How does the information in "Practice, Practice, Practice" relate to this sentence? Use
two details from the passage to support your answer.

_____

_____

_____

_____

_____

10   The author suggests choosing to learn a language of a country or culture you are interested in. Explain how this could be motivating.

_____

_____

_____

_____

_____

11   In the section titled "Ignore the Myths," the author describes how some people say that babies learn more quickly than adults. How does the author show that this is untrue? Use **two** details from the passage to support your response.

_____

_____

_____

_____

_____

12 Describe **two** reasons that long study sessions are not a good idea.

1: _____

_____

2: _____

_____

13 Compare the information in the sections "Don't Compare Yourself" and "Measure Your Progress in Bigger Blocks." Explain how the ideas in the two sections are similar.

_____

_____

_____

_____

_____

14 In the last paragraph, the author refers to your "quest to learn a new language." What does the word *quest* suggest about learning a language? Explain your answer.

_____

_____

_____

_____

_____

15   One problem people face when trying to learn a new language is staying positive and motivated. Describe **three** tips the author gives that could help people stay positive and motivated. Use details from the passage to support your response.

_____

_____

_____

_____

_____

_____

_____

_____

_____

_____

_____

_____

_____

_____

_____

_____

_____

_____

Practice Set 16

Opinion Piece

It's Time for an Allowance

Instructions

This set has one passage for you to read. The passage is followed by questions.

Read each question carefully. For each multiple choice question, fill in the circle for the correct answer. For other types of questions, follow the instructions given. Some of the questions require a written answer. Write your answer on the lines provided.

It's Time for an Allowance

Dear Mom and Dad,

I would like to ask you a question. I know that at home my brothers, sisters, and I have everything we need. However, I would like to ask for an allowance. I have talked to my friends at school and many of them have allowances. If I had an allowance, I could learn to budget money. I would not have to ask you for money and you could take my allowance away if I broke house rules or got bad grades in school. I think it is also a good idea because I can become more responsible with money. Sometimes I need things and I would be able to buy them myself.

I think the perfect age for giving children allowances is 10. At 10 years old, many children have allowances. An allowance can also include the money that parents give their children for lunch money at school. This is a good idea for me because I like to buy a lot of snacks at school. If you gave me an allowance for the whole week, I would have to buy fewer snacks if I wanted to buy something else. Sometimes I want to buy a new game or books, but I have to wait until Christmas or my birthday. If I had an allowance for the whole week that included my lunch money I could learn to budget so that I can get something I really want.

Everybody has to make a budget. I know that you have a budget every month. You have to see how much you make in the month and then decide what you can afford to buy. I think that many of my friends' parents have budgets too. I know that having a budget is a good skill to have because when I get older and make my own money, I will need to know how to keep a budget.

Whenever I need something, I usually go to Mom to ask her for money. If I had an allowance I wouldn't have to ask Mom when I need or want to buy something for myself. Sometimes I want to buy something at the grocery store, but Mom says we can't buy it this week. I could buy my own favorite cookies or cereal with my allowance too. I also like to play games and I could learn to save money to buy games too. If I want to buy something big, I would have to save the money to buy it. I can learn to budget and save money at the same time.

Having an allowance would help to teach me how to manage my money and make my own decisions.

As my parents, you can decide if I get my allowance each week. For example, if I break house rules or get a bad grade on a test, you can take away my allowance. As you know, I don't like to do house chores. However, having an allowance would change this! I would complete my chores faster because I wouldn't want to risk losing my allowance! I am happy to earn my allowance, and we can even decide on what chores I need to do together. Instead of trying to get out of chores, I would do them happily because I would understand that I am earning my allowance.

If you gave me an allowance, I could even buy something for my sisters and brothers. I know that I wouldn't buy something for them every week, but I could buy my little sister new socks or a new stuffed animal. Maybe we could go to the arcade at the mall on Friday once in a while too. I think that since I am the oldest I should be the first to get an allowance. After I get my allowance, my brothers and sisters can get an allowance too when they turn 10. I'm already 11, so my brothers and sisters would even have their allowance longer than me. That isn't even fair, but I would accept it and not grumble or whine.

Lastly, if I had an allowance I could put money in the poor box at church and support other charities that I think are important. Sometimes at school, we have a food drive to collect food for people that don't have enough to eat. If I had an allowance, I could learn to save money so that I could buy the food myself for the food drive. I would really be giving to others instead of just asking you to give to others!

I think that having an allowance is a really good idea for all these reasons. I can learn to budget money, I can learn to save money, and I can even give money to others. If I had an allowance, I also wouldn't keep nagging you to give me money for something or to buy me something. We would all be happier. You should also feel good knowing that I am learning the good money skills that everybody needs in life. I hope that you will consider this carefully and agree with me. I feel certain that I am ready for this and old enough to be responsible with money.

Thank you,

Frederica

1   Which sentence from the first paragraph tells Frederica's main purpose for writing the letter?

  Ⓐ   *I would like to ask you a question.*

  Ⓑ   *I know that at home my brothers, sisters, and I have everything we need.*

  Ⓒ   *However, I would like to ask for an allowance.*

  Ⓓ   *I have talked to my friends at school and many of them have allowances.*

2   Read this sentence from the passage.

  I think the perfect age for giving children allowances is 10.

  As it is used in the sentence, which word means about the same as *perfect*?

  Ⓐ   early

  Ⓑ   ideal

  Ⓒ   usual

  Ⓓ   wrong

3   Look at the art at the bottom of the first page and read the caption. The caption supports the idea that having an allowance would make Frederica more –

  Ⓐ   generous

  Ⓑ   responsible

  Ⓒ   hardworking

  Ⓓ   patient

4   Read this sentence from the passage.

> **That isn't even fair, but I would accept it and not grumble or whine.**

What do the words *grumble* and *whine* refer to?

Ⓐ   complaining

Ⓑ   fighting

Ⓒ   planning

Ⓓ   spending

5   Read these sentences from the last paragraph.

> **I think that having an allowance is a really good idea for all these reasons. I can learn to budget money, I can learn to save money, and I can even give money to others.**

Which sentence best describes the second sentence above?

Ⓐ   It is a summary of the author's reasons.

Ⓑ   It is an example to support the author's point.

Ⓒ   It is a list of facts about having an allowance.

Ⓓ   It is background information on the topic.

6   Use the information from the first paragraph to complete the web below with **three** benefits to the author of having an allowance.

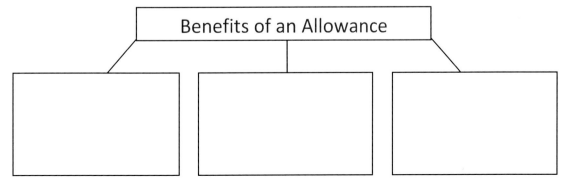

Benefits of an Allowance

7   Frederica wants to replace the first sentence with a sentence that better describes the main idea of her letter. Which sentence would Frederica be best to use?

    Ⓐ   It is not fair that everyone else my age has an allowance.

    Ⓑ   It would be great for all of us if I had an allowance.

    Ⓒ   Having an allowance is one important way that kids learns about money.

    Ⓓ   We sometimes argue about money, and an allowance would solve that.

8   Summarize the example the author gives in paragraph 2 to show how she would have to make choices about how to spend her allowance. Use **two** details from the paragraph in your answer.

_____

_____

_____

_____

_____

9   How does paragraph 3 show that having an allowance would help create money skills for life? Use **two** details from the paragraph in your answer.

_____

_____

_____

_____

10 The art on the last page of the passages shows a family deciding on what chores everyone does. What does the art suggest about how the kids feel about doing chores? How does this support the ideas in the paragraph next to the art?

_____

_____

_____

_____

_____

11 Describe **two** ways the passage suggests that Frederica is generous and thoughtful.

1: _____

_____

2: _____

_____

12 Frederica states that her parents can decide if she gets her allowance each week. Complete the table by listing **two** more reasons that Frederica gives for her parents choosing not to give her the allowance.

Reasons Not to Receive the Allowance

1) not doing her chores
2)
3)

13   Describe **one** way that giving Frederica an allowance would make life easier for the parents. Use **two** details from the passage to support your response.

_____

_____

_____

_____

_____

14   Read this sentence from the passage.

> **If I had an allowance I also wouldn't keep nagging you to give me money for something.**

What does the word _nagging_ suggest about how the parents feel about Frederica asking for money? Explain how this helps support Frederica's argument.

_____

_____

_____

_____

_____

15 Frederica states that having an allowance would help her "become more responsible with money." How does Frederica support this idea? Use **three** details from the passage in your response.

_____

_____

_____

_____

_____

_____

_____

_____

_____

_____

_____

_____

_____

_____

_____

_____

_____

_____

Practice Set 17

History Article

The Discovery of Gold in California

Instructions

This set has one passage for you to read. The passage is followed by questions.

Read each question carefully. For each multiple choice question, fill in the circle for the correct answer. For other types of questions, follow the instructions given. Some of the questions require a written answer. Write your answer on the lines provided.

The Discovery of Gold in California
Adapted from *The Story of American History* by Albert F. Blaisdell, 1902

In 1847, California had a population of less than 10,000 people. Then a remarkable event occurred. Captain Sutter had settled on the Sacramento River and built a sawmill. In January, 1848, one of Sutter's laborers, by the name of Marshall, while digging a ditch for the mill, found shiny pieces of yellow metal which they suspected might be gold.

"I wonder what that yellow stuff is," said he. "I wonder if it is gold."

"I reckon it is brass," said one of his helpers.

"Let me try vinegar on it," said Marshall. It was tried and the vinegar did not affect the "yellow stuff."

The men threw down their tools and went to work searching for gold. Mr. Sutter laughed at the idea. But gold indeed it was, and there was plenty of it!

The news spread. Soon everybody knew that pure gold was found and in wonderful quantities. What a rush there was to the "diggings"! How all sorts of people from all over the Western coast crowded in! Doctors left their sick, ministers their pulpits, traders their shops, mechanics their tools, and farmers their fields, all half frantic with the desire to dig their fortunes out of the golden sands of California.

When the news of the discovery of gold reached the East, many people seemed to catch the contagion. Multitudes started at once for California. Thousands came by long wagon trains over the dreary plains. Vast numbers came from foreign countries and struggled through long journeys by sea. Even the crews and often the officers abandoned the ships that brought crowds to the Pacific coast and started for the gold "diggings."

The rush to the gold fields began in 1848, but became enormous in 1849. Those who went that year are since called "Forty-niners." There were over eighty thousand of them! The crowds that thronged the gold regions dug up the country for miles around Sutter's mill. They tore up his beautiful valley and ruined his farm. But they soon learned that gold was also to be found in larger quantities along the streams, among the mountains, and in valleys.

Month by month new-comers swarmed in, and the excitement grew more intense. Some found prizes, nuggets of solid gold as large as an acorn or a walnut, and at times masses two or three pounds in weight. However much gold a man found, he was wildly eager to get more.

A great deal of suffering ensued from the scarcity of food and the enormous prices of everything. Potatoes sold for a dollar apiece, eggs at the same price, wood at fifty dollars a cord, and flour at a hundred dollars a barrel. Large butcher knives were found very useful for digging, and brought thirty dollars each. A dose of the cheapest medicine cost five dollars, and a physician's visit a hundred dollars.

Money was not used at the mines, but in its place the ore itself, or "dust," at about sixteen dollars an ounce. Miners carried small scales, weighed their gold dust, and paid their bills with it.

At the rough log tavern: "What do you charge for dinner here?" "Half an ounce."

At the wayside store: "What's the price of these boots?" "Three ounces."

In seven years' time, from 1849 to 1856, the gold found in California was worth nearly five hundred million dollars!

Eventually, gold became harder to find. The many people who had come to quickly make their fortunes moved on to other opportunities. However, California had been changed forever.

California is still rich in its gold, but it is still richer in its wonderful climate and its marvelous scenery; in the wealth of its grain fields; its sheep and cattle; its orange groves and its vineyards. These make California the real land of gold, and ensure the prosperity and happiness of its people.

1 Read this sentence from the passage.

The men threw down their tools and went to work searching for gold.

The phrase "threw down their tools" suggests that the men were –

Ⓐ   angry

Ⓑ   enthusiastic

Ⓒ   tired

Ⓓ   uncertain

2 Read these sentences from the passage.

The men threw down their tools and went to work searching for gold. Mr. Sutter laughed at the idea.

What is the most likely reason Mr. Sutter laughed?

Ⓐ   He did not believe it was gold.

Ⓑ   He did not think gold was worth much.

Ⓒ   He was more interested in his sawmill.

Ⓓ   He thought it was his gold because it was on his land.

3 Paragraph 6 states that gold was found "in wonderful quantities." What does this statement mean?

Ⓐ   The gold was of high quality.

Ⓑ   The gold was easy to find.

Ⓒ   There was competition to find the gold.

Ⓓ   There was a large amount of gold.

4   Select the **two** sentences that best show that damage was done by all the mining activity.

☐   The rush to the gold fields began in 1848, but became enormous in 1849.

☐   Those who went that year are since called "Forty-niners."

☐   There were over eighty thousand of them!

☐   The crowds that thronged the gold regions dug up the country for miles around Sutter's mill.

☐   They tore up his beautiful valley and ruined his farm.

☐   But they soon learned that gold was also to be found in larger quantities along the streams, among the mountains, and in valleys.

5   Read this sentence from the passage.

However much gold a man found, he was wildly eager to get more.

This sentence mainly implies that people were –

Ⓐ   cowardly

Ⓑ   determined

Ⓒ   greedy

Ⓓ   impatient

6   Use the details given in the passage to complete the chart with the missing cost of each item.

Item	Cost
Potatoes	$1 per piece
Eggs	
Wood	$50 per cord
Flour	
Butcher knives	
Medicine	at least $5
Physician's visit	

7   Read these sentences from the passage.

Money was not used at the mines, but in its place the ore itself, or "dust," at about sixteen dollars an ounce. Miners carried small scales, weighed their gold dust, and paid their bills with it.

At the rough log tavern: "What do you charge for dinner here?" "Half an ounce."

At the wayside store: "What's the price of these boots?" "Three ounces."

Which term best describes these sentences?

Ⓐ   an anecdote

Ⓑ   an argument

Ⓒ   an opinion

Ⓓ   a metaphor

8   How can you tell that the discovery of gold was an accident? Use **two** details from the passage to support your answer.

_____

_____

_____

_____

_____

9   Paragraphs 2, 3, and 4 describe a conversation between Marshall and his helpers. What does the conversation describe Marshall doing? Use **two** details from the passage to support your answer.

_____

_____

_____

_____

_____

10   Paragraph 6 states that "all sorts of people from all over the Western coast crowded in." How does the author support this statement? Use details from the paragraph to support your answer.

_____

_____

_____

_____

_____

11   List **two** details from the passage that emphasize that people traveled a long way to try to find gold in California.

1: _____

_____

2: _____

_____

12   How many Forty-niners traveled to California? How does this compare to the original population of California? Explain your answer.

_____

_____

_____

_____

_____

13 The last paragraph suggests that agriculture is more important to California than gold. List **four** types of agriculture mentioned in the last paragraph.

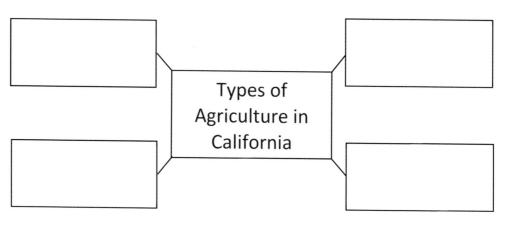

Types of Agriculture in California

14 Select the statement the author of the passage would most likely agree with. Then explain why you selected that statement. Use **two** details from the passage to support your answer.

☐ It was worth it to travel to California to try to find gold.

☐ It was not worth it to travel to California to try to find gold.

_____

_____

_____

_____

_____

15   How does the author help readers understand the excitement of the gold rush? Use at least **three** details from the passage to support your answer.

_____

_____

_____

_____

_____

_____

_____

_____

_____

_____

_____

_____

_____

_____

_____

_____

Practice Set 18

Interview

Interview with Abraham Lincoln

Instructions

This set has one passage for you to read. The passage is followed by questions.

Read each question carefully. For each multiple choice question, fill in the circle for the correct answer. For other types of questions, follow the instructions given. Some of the questions require a written answer. Write your answer on the lines provided.

Interview with Abraham Lincoln

A lady by the name of Cindy Kennedy traveled back in time to interview Abraham Lincoln in 1860. Below is that interview.

Cindy: Hi, Mr. President. It is nice to meet you!

Lincoln: Hi, Cindy. Thank you for traveling to the capital to interview me.

Cindy: Oh, you bet, sir! My first question is: Did you ever invent anything?

Lincoln: Actually, yes! I invented and patented a device that helped steamboats that accidentally ran ashore.

Cindy: Wow! Did you go to school for science and engineering?

Lincoln: No, actually. I had never studied science or engineering at all. In fact, I only had eighteen months of formal education before becoming a lawyer.

Cindy: Oh! Did you go to school for that?

Lincoln: (*laughs*) I did not. But, that can be our little secret. (*winks*)

Cindy: You got it, sir! Do you hunt like other presidents before you?

Lincoln: No, I love animals!

Cindy: What about fishing?

Lincoln: Cindy! Fish are animals, too!

Cindy: Oh! You are right, sir. Do you play any sports? Do you play basketball, by chance?

Lincoln: What? What is basketball? I've never heard of it.

Cindy starts to turn red. She had forgotten that basketball was not invented until 1891. She quickly thinks of a way to cover her mistake.

Cindy: It's a new game I heard about. It helps to be tall to play it. But I guess it is not known about here yet. So, what sport do you play?

Lincoln: I wrestle! Well, before I became president, I wrestled.

Cindy: That's amazing! Do you think that is the most interesting thing about you?

Lincoln: Actually, I think the most interesting thing about me is the fact that I have no middle name! I am simply Abraham Lincoln.

Cindy: Incredible! What is your favorite food?

Lincoln: Honestly, it is a three-way tie between oysters, chicken casserole, and fruit.

Cindy: You can keep the oysters, but, fruit? Any particular kind?

Lincoln: Nope, any kind will do!

Cindy: Interesting... Some Presidents were known to have their dog served next to the dining table in the White House. Was your dog permitted to eat next to the table?

Lincoln: Of course! I needed Fido to pick up my scraps. It was actually the cat who received the most interesting service.

Cindy: How so?

Lincoln: Tabby, my cat, dines at the table with the family!

Cindy: Oh, wow! Now, can I call you Abe?

Lincoln: Oh goodness, no. I despise being called Abe. Abraham is fine, but Lincoln is preferable. It sounds more professional.

Cindy: Oh! How is Mr. President or President Lincoln?

Lincoln: Those are fine as well...

Cindy: Perfect. So, about your hat...

Lincoln: Yes, what about it?

Cindy: It is rumored that you keep papers in that tall hat of yours. Is that true?

Lincoln: (*sighs*) Yes... I keep my most important documents in there. But, I'm not going to tell you which ones.

Cindy: Fair enough. Earlier you said you like animals –

Lincoln: Love.

Cindy: Pardon?

Lincoln: You said *like*, and I truthfully *love* them.

Cindy: My apologies. You said you *love* animals. Which animal is your favor –

Lincoln: Cats. Definitely cats.

Cindy: (*laughs*) Alright, cats are your favorite! Now, let's ask a serious question. What would you like to do as president to change the lives of people?

Lincoln: Well, I do think that women should have the right to vote. However, that is not a popular idea. Many people aren't ready for that change. In fact, I might not be president much longer if people found out how I felt. So that can stay between us Miss Cindy, if you do not mind.

Cindy: Of course, Mr. President. Now, you are quite well-known for your beard. What convinced you to grow a beard?

Lincoln: An 11-year-old girl wrote me a letter telling me that women were more likely to trust a man with a beard than a man without a beard.

Cindy: So, you grew your beard out based on advice from an eleven-year-old? Seriously?

Lincoln: Of course. She made a compelling argument.

Cindy: You may not realize this yet, but you have set a lot of records as president. You were the only president to hold a patent and the tallest. What else are you the first of?

Lincoln: Well, I was the first to be photographed, instead of painted, at my presidential ceremony.

Cindy: That is incredible. Well, that is all the time I have today, Mr. President. Thank you for meeting me!

Lincoln: It was my pleasure Cindy.

1   Read this statement from the interview.

Cindy: Oh, you bet, sir! My first question is: Did you ever invent anything?

The words "you bet, sir" mainly make Cindy seem –

Ⓐ   curious

Ⓑ   excited

Ⓒ   nervous

Ⓓ   relaxed

2   Why does Cindy turn red right after she asks about basketball?

Ⓐ   She is angry.

Ⓑ   She is confused.

Ⓒ   She is tired.

Ⓓ   She is embarrassed.

3   Based on your answer to Question 2, explain why Cindy feels that way. Use details from the passage to explain your answer.

_____

_____

_____

_____

_____

4   When asked about his favorite food, Lincoln says that it is "a three-way tie between oysters, chicken casserole, and fruit." What does Lincoln mean by this?

Ⓐ   He likes all three foods equally.

Ⓑ   He eats all three foods together.

Ⓒ   He has one food at each of three meals.

Ⓓ   He prefers the foods in the order listed.

5   Based on details in the interview, list **four** names Lincoln considers it suitable to call him.

1. _____

2. _____

3. _____

4. _____

6   Read this statement from the interview.

Cindy: So, you grew your beard out based on advice from an eleven-year-old? Seriously?

How would Cindy most likely sound when saying this?

Ⓐ   surprised

Ⓑ   puzzled

Ⓒ   bored

Ⓓ   annoyed

7   Which answer given by Lincoln represents changing technology at the time that he was interviewed?

Ⓐ   **Lincoln**: No, actually. I had never studied science or engineering at all. In fact, I only had eighteen months of formal education before becoming a lawyer.

Ⓑ   **Lincoln:** Actually, I think the most interesting thing about me is the fact that I have no middle name! I am simply Abraham Lincoln.

Ⓒ   **Lincoln:** An 11-year-old girl wrote me a letter telling me that women were more likely to trust a man with a beard than a man without a beard.

Ⓓ   **Lincoln:** Well, I was the first to be photographed, instead of painted, at my presidential ceremony.

8   When Lincoln describes how he invented a device to help steamboats, Cindy asks about his education. How does his answer help show that inventing the device was an impressive achievement? Explain your answer.

_____

_____

_____

_____

9   Read the answer that Lincoln gives when asked whether he studied to be a lawyer.

Lincoln: (*laughs*) I did not. But, that can be our little secret. (*winks*)

List the **two** actions described in the statement and describe how they help show how Lincoln feels about not studying law.

_____

_____

_____

_____

10   Does Lincoln enjoy fishing? In your answer, explain how you can tell.

_____

_____

_____

_____

_____

11   Why does Lincoln correct Cindy when she mentions him liking animals? In your answer, explain what Lincoln wants Cindy to understand about him.

_____

_____

_____

_____

_____

12   List **two** details given that show that Lincoln prefers cats over dogs.

1: _____

_____

2: _____

_____

13   In the interview, Lincoln gives his opinion on women voting. Why does Lincoln ask Cindy to keep his opinion just between them? Use details from the passage in your answer.

_____

_____

_____

_____

14   How does Lincoln look in the photograph in the passage? Is this similar or different to how he seems in the interview? Explain your answer.

_____

_____

_____

_____

15 Cindy asks Lincoln a wide range of questions, but does not ask many serious questions. If you were able to travel back in time, what three questions would you want to ask Lincoln? In your answer, explain why you would want to ask each question.

Answer Key

Ben Franklin's Experiments

Question	Answer
1	C
2	B
3	C
4	D
5	kite, key, string, silk ribbon
6	scientist, inventor
7	A
8	D
9	The student should make a reasonable inference about what might have happened if Franklin had not used the silk. The answer could describe how he may have had a huge shock, how all the electricity could have reached him, or how he could have been seriously hurt.
10	The student should list how the church steeple was high up in the sky like the kite was and how the steeple was made of metal like the key was.
11	The student should identify that Franklin got an electric shock when he touched the key. The student should explain that this proved that lightning is electrical current.
12	The student should describe how Franklin's experiment encouraged other scientists and inventors to find ways to use electricity to make light.
13	The student should make a reasonable inference about what the kite invention shows about Franklin's creativity. The answer could refer to how he used his creativity to solve a problem or how his invention was creative.
14	The student should relate Franklin's creativity to the list of inventions given in the passage. The student may describe how his invention of the kite and key device helps show he used his creativity to solve problems and invent new things.
15	The student should write an essay showing that the experiment was dangerous and use relevant supporting details from the passage. The student may refer to how powerful lightning is, how he could have received a much greater electrical shock, Priestley's warning about how each bolt of lightning "gives off as much energy as a ton of dynamite," or how many people agreed that Franklin was lucky he only got an electric shock.

The Life of Walt Disney

Question	Answer
1	C
2	Walt Disney, Roy Disney/Walt's brother Roy, Ub Iwerks
3	B
4	A
5	1937 – Snow White and the Seven Dwarfs 1964 – Mary Poppins
6	B
7	D
8	D
9	The student should list how he contributed his work to the school newspaper and how he sold his work to neighbors.
10	F, O, F, O, F, O
11	The student may list how Roy got Walt his first job in an art studio, how Walt moved with Roy to Hollywood, or how Roy and Walt started Disney Brothers' Studio together.
12	The student should describe how *Steamboat Willie* launched Mickey Mouse. The student may refer to the success and popularity of Mickey Mouse, or to how the success of the cartoon led to the creation of more characters, cartoons, and films.
13	The student should describe how Mickey Mouse was the first real success for Walt Disney and his company. The student may refer to Walt's failed businesses before this, or to the many successes that came after this.
14	B
15	The student should give a reasonable explanation of what Walt Disney's life can teach people about never giving up and use relevant supporting details from the passage. The student may refer to Walt's early business failures, Walt's eventual successes, how Walt kept trying new things, or how Walt pushed for new ideas like Disneyland even when other people did not believe in them.

A Review of *Inside Out*

Question	Answer
1	B
2	Unlike other animated movies, *Inside Out* is not about an adventure, romance, historical fiction event, or even a trip into space.
3	The student should list any four of the reasons below. Riley misses her old school, Riley misses her friends, Riley misses her hockey team, Riley doesn't like the new house, Riley's father works too much, or Riley dislikes the pizza restaurant
4	A
5	B
6	B
7	The student should list any two of the features below about each character. Joy is happy and bubbly. Joy has bright blue hair. Joy has a big smile. Anger is red. Anger is square-shaped. Anger has flames shoot out of his head. Sadness is blue. Sadness has a frown on her face. Sadness sometimes cries.
8	The student should complete the diagram with the details below. happy / feels good when she talks about her old life sad / remembers how far away her old school and friends are
9	The student should list any three of the examples below. how and why people feel emotions, how memory works, how and why people respond to events the way they do, or how people feel emotions
10	The student should identify that Riley's islands are family, honesty, hockey, and goofiness. The student should explain that the islands are the things that are important to Riley and that she is not happy without them.
11	The student should explain that the comparison would probably emphasize how happy she was in Minnesota compared to how unhappy she is in her new home.
12	The student should relate the art of the people's faces showing different emotions to the movie. The student should explain how the art shows how people feel many different emotions and how the movie explores the emotions that Riley feels.
13	The student should identify that the paragraph describes the film as funny and refers to people laughing. The answer should show an understanding that the rest of the review does not show that the film is funny.
14	The student should give a reasonable explanation of why the film is titled *Inside Out*. The answer should refer to how the emotions that are felt on the inside are represented as real characters.
15	The student should give a reasonable description of what makes the movie unique and different and use relevant supporting details from the passage. The answer should refer to how emotions are represented as real characters.

Baking Bread: From Basics to Brilliance

Question	Answer
1	A
2	Dry yeast Sugar Salt Olive oil Olives
3	B
4	The student should list how the arrows show adding the olives to the bread or mixing the olives into the bread and how the arrows show the steps to do in order.
5	The student should identify that Step 3 would be different and explain that you would mix in different things in this step.
6	The student should explain that bread goes from "basics to brilliance" by adding in other ingredients to make a special type of bread. The answer should refer to olive bread as being a special bread or describe how adding the olives makes the bread more than just a basic bread.

Ladder Safety

Question	Answer
1	C
2	B
3	Rule 4
4	The student should describe how the photograph shows someone using a ladder to do a job around the home. The answer should refer to the photograph as an example of ladder use or as showing that ladders are useful tools.
5	The student should give a reasonable explanation of how the illustration shows the importance of wearing a tool belt. The answer may refer to how the tools are safely stored or how the person's hands are free to use to climb the ladder.
6	The student should list two reasons it is important not to rush based on the information in the instructions. The answer could refer to doing checks before using the ladder, to transporting it carefully, to placing it correctly, or to making sure it is secure.

Finding Your Fluffy Friend

Question	Answer
1	C
2	Step 2
3	The student should describe how the author explains that cats often wander and explore but do return home, and how cats may be just lazing somewhere.
4	The student should describe how the first four steps all involve checking certain places for your cat or how the first four steps all refer to common places missing cats could be.
5	The student should identify that the illustrations are light-hearted and give a reasonable description of the illustrations as support. The answer may refer to the illustrations overall as being cartoonish or showing funny cats, or could refer to specific illustrations such as the cat with the "I AM LOST" sign or the cat sitting on the tree.
6	The student should list putting your name and phone number on a missing poster or attention notice and putting your name and phone number on the cat's collar.

Find What You Love

Question	Answer
1	D
2	The student should complete the diagram with the details listed below. slept on his friends' dorm room floors, returned bottles to earn money to buy food, walked 7 miles every Sunday to get a good meal
3	B
4	D
5	D
6	The student should complete the table with either Pixar or NeXT and list the information below for the business selected. NeXT: grew to 500 employees, Apple bought it for over $400 million Pixar: *Toy Story* made over $350 million, Pixar is the world's most successful animation studio
7	The student should list how the parents Steve was first meant for could have accepted a boy and how Steve's biological mother could have not signed the adoption papers because his parents had not gone to college.
8	The student should explain that Steve felt bad about, guilty about, or worried about the high costs for his parents. The student should describe how this was one of the reasons that Steve dropped out of college.
9	The student should explain that dropping out gave Steve the freedom to attend whatever classes interested him instead of having to do set classes whether they interested him or not.
10	The student should identify that this statement did not remain true. The student should describe how Steve ended up using what he learned about calligraphy when he was designing the Macintosh computer.
11	The student should explain that Steve was very upset at the time but now considers it a positive thing. The answer may refer to how Steve describes how he was devastated, disappointed, and confused, but later says it was "the best thing that could have ever happened to me."
12	The student should relate the quote about looking forward instead of looking back to Steve's actions after leaving Apple. The answer should refer to how Steve started working again and started two new companies.
13	The student should compare Steve after being fired from Apple to Steve after dropping out of college. The answer should identify that both situations allowed him the freedom to be creative, try new things, and explore.
14	Find your passion.
15	The student should give a reasonable explanation of how loving what he did helped Steve during difficult times and use relevant supporting details. The answer should refer to how loving what he did helped him after he was fired from Apple and allowed him to keep working and achieve new things.

Discovery Elementary's Fundraising Festival

Question	Answer
1	A
2	D
3	upbeat music, colorful decorations
4	A
5	The student should complete the table with any three of the examples below. Thailand – mango sticky rice / Germany – sausage with yellow mustard / Mexico – fried ice cream / Lebanon – chickpea hummus / Bulgaria – chicken kebabs / America – caramel apples, hotdogs, or pretzels
6	starting a pet program
7	The student should circle any three of the phrases below. craziest outfit / go wild / crazy hairstyles / get clownish / bright and colorful clothes / be artsy / shows off your imagination
8	A
9	The student may list how the author says that every dollar spent will go to the school, how the author says that the money will make the school "the best grade school in the county," or how the author tells readers how the money will be spent.
10	The student should explain that the sentences tell how the festival will raise money or what students need to do to donate to the festival.
11	The student should give a reasonable explanation of how the festival will offer something for everyone and use relevant supporting details. The answer could refer to the wide range of foods available or the statement that there will be vegetarian, dairy-free, and gluten free options.
12	The student should identify that the teachers want to spend the money on technology. The answer should refer to how the teachers want to purchase laptops and electronic whiteboards.
13	The student may list how the author says that "we need all of you to come together," how the author says that help is needed for the school to reach its goals, how the author tells people to "be the change you want to see in your school," or how the author says that "we can't do it without you."
14	The student should compare the three prizes and should identify that the first prize benefits a whole class while the second and third prizes are just for the individual.
15	The student should give an opinion on whether the festival is a clever way to raise money and use relevant details to support the opinion. The student could argue either way, as long as the opinion is explained well and supported.

How to Help the Earth Stay Healthy

Question	Answer
1	C
2	B
3	lights, air conditioner, television, computer
4	C
5	open a window, spray yourself with water, drink lots of water
6	A
7	D
8	Everyone can make a difference.
9	The student should explain that the art represents how healthy the planet is. The student should relate the art to the main idea of what people can do to help the Earth stay healthy.
10	television / leave it on in the background / turn it off when not in use computer / leave it to shut itself down / shut it down when you have finished
11	The student should list how fans use less energy and how fans can be used to cool down a small space instead of a huge area.
12	The student should explain that people can look for items displaying the Energy Star symbol and know that they are a smart choice or a choice that is good for the environment. The answer may refer to how people do not have to look at data themselves and how this makes it easy for people to shop smart.
13	The student should list how people can recycle goods instead of throwing them away and how people can buy items that can be reused.
14	The student should describe the change as being to stop using plastic grocery bags that are just thrown out and to start using reusable bags instead. The student should give a reasonable explanation of whether the change would be easy to make.
15	The student should describe three examples from the passage of balancing what people want with what is right for the environment. The answer may refer to use electricity smartly and without wasting it, using alternatives to air conditioning to stay cool, making smart choices when buying appliances, recycling goods, choosing to use reusable items around the house, or swapping plastic grocery bags for reusable bags.

Save the Park

Question	Answer
1	I want to ask for your help to clean up our town's park and river.
2	B
3	D
4	C
5	The student should list putting an article in the local newspaper, putting posters on town noticeboards, and giving out flyers.
6	C
7	The student should list how Mr. Sanchez will help make the mural design and how Miss Williams will help make the posters and flyers.
8	C
9	The student should describe how Annie used to visit the park with her mother often and enjoy spending time there, but how she no longer visits the park.
10	The student should give a reasonable description of how the photograph would make readers feel and state an opinion on whether it would encourage readers to want to clean up the park.
11	The student should list a mural, a children's playground, and exercise equipment.
12	The student may list how Ms. Gonzales gave Annie advice on asking the mayor, made writing the letter to the mayor part of class work, feels excited about the project, or has offered to be project manager.
13	The student should explain that Annie wants to put a letter in the local newspaper to raise money, request help, or get people to make donations. The answer may refer to raising money from the community or to the description of what will be included in the article.
14	The student should give a reasonable explanation of how the photograph creates hope. The answer may refer to how the photograph shows how great the park could look, how the park would be popular, or it may refer to the caption describing the park as a "lovely place that people want to be."
15	The student should describe three ways that Annie is encouraging others to help or getting people involved in the project. The answer may refer to involving her classmates, involving her brother and his classmates, getting the support and help of teachers, asking for the mayor's help, or her plans to raise money and request help from the community.

Interview with Valarie Smyth, Former Peace Corps Volunteer

Question	Answer
1	D
2	President John F. Kennedy 1961 over 140 countries
3	D
4	Colombia – build bridges Uganda – work with sick children Thailand – start a sports team
5	B
6	B
7	B
8	C
9	The student should list how she loved giving back and how she loved learning about new cultures.
10	The student should relate Valarie's experience volunteering in Mexico to her decision to join the Peace Corps. The answer should refer to how the Peace Corps would allow her to visit other countries to help people and to learn about new cultures for free.
11	The student should explain that people can study whatever interests them. The answer may refer to how the Peace Corps can use many different types of skills or how people will be given a role that suits their skills and education.
12	The student should list how Valarie taught English before in Mexico and how she studied teaching in college.
13	The student should explain that the question is not important to the main idea of the interview. The answer should show an understanding that the rest of the interview is about joining the Peace Corps or being a Peace Corps volunteer, while this question is about something more trivial.
14	The student should complete the diagram with any three benefits of being a Peace Corps volunteer mentioned in the second last answer. The student may list being able to see the world, making a difference to others, learning new skills, learning new languages, making lifelong friends, having amazing stories to tell, or being respected by others.
15	The student should give a reasonable description of three challenges of being in the Peace Corps and use relevant supporting details. The answer could refer to having to live in a foreign country, having to learn a new language, being away from family and friends, having to do challenging tasks, being very busy, or any other reasonable challenge or difficulty.

The First Olympic Games – They Sure Have Changed!

Question	Answer
1	B
2	C
3	C
4	The student should select the boxes listed below. boxing – next; chariot races – last; discus – last; javelin – last; running – first; wrestling – next
5	Different people run so far and hand off the torch to a new runner. Then this runner runs and then gives the torch to another runner.
6	D
7	The student should explain that both the first Olympics and the Olympics today are about competing peacefully.
8	The student should explain that women were first allowed to compete at the Paris Olympics of 1900 and were unable to compete before that time.
9	The student should list how each color represents one of the five continents competing and how the rings are all connected.
10	The similarity listed could be that winners receive some form of award or that winners are treated like heroes or superstars when they return home. The difference listed could be that winners today receive medals and flowers instead of a crown of leaves or that winners today may also receive money and gifts from their country.
11	The student should explain that the photograph shows the Olympic Torch lighting the cauldron. The answer should describe how the torch is lit in Greece and travels to the host city for the lighting of the flame on opening day.
12	The student should explain that the first country is always Greece and that the last country is always the host country.
13	The student may list how the Olympic flag is handed to the mayor of the next host city, how the flag of the next host country is raised, how the song or anthem of the next host country is sung, or how the closing performance shows the next host city.
14	The student should describe how the modern Olympics honors how the Olympics began in Greece. The answer could refer to how it is still about competing peacefully, how the torch is lit in Greece and travels to the host country, or how Greece always marches first in the Closing Ceremony.
15	The student should describe three ways the Olympics have changed and include relevant supporting details. The answer may refer to there being more events, to it involving more countries, to it being held in different countries, how women are now able to compete, or to the rewards that winning athletes receive.

Bake Sale

Question	Answer
1	B
2	A
3	Day – Saturday Date – February 14 Time – 2 to 6 p.m. Location – Green Street Town Library
4	A
5	The student should identify that the letters of the words "Bake Sale" look like cookies, and relate this to the flyer as being about a sale of baked goods like cookies.
6	The student should describe details that suggest that the goods purchased would make suitable Valentine's Day gifts. The answer may refer to the photograph of the boxed heart-shaped cookies, the detail on the flyer about gift wrapping, or the detail on the flyer about adding a gift card with a special message.

Summer Art Workshop

Question	Answer
1	A
2	C
3	The student should list T-shirt painting, spray painting, face painting, and glass painting.
4	Pottery Yoga
5	The student should explain that the workshop offers activities other than art activities. The student should support the answer by giving examples of activities that are not art-related such as singing, water fun, and yoga. The answer could also refer to the illustrations of people swimming, sailing, and exercising.
6	The student should provide a reasonable comparison of the activities for the 3 to 7 age group and the 13 to 16 age group. The answer may refer to the activities for the 13 to 16 age group as being more serious, more difficult, or more educational.

Josie's Guitar Lessons

Question	Answer
1	D
2	B
3	B
4	A
5	The student should identify that the cost is presented on a price tag. The answer may refer to how it is clever to have the price on a tag hanging from the word *lessons*.
6	The student should explain that the classes being available for beginner, moderate, and expert levels supports the idea that the classes suit students with different amounts of experience.
7	The student should relate how Josie experienced playing music in her childhood and developed a love of music to Josie wanting to start her business to share her passion with young people and inspire young people to learn to play music like she did.

Belgian Waffles

Question	Answer
1	A
2	D
3	An easier option is to buy waffles ready to go.
4	The student should list how you can have them for different meals and how you can top them with many different things.
5	The student should identify that Belgian waffles are compared to pancakes and doughnuts. The student should give a reasonable explanation of why the comparisons are made, such as to help people imagine what waffles taste like or to help readers understand waffles by showing how they are similar to more common food items.
6	The student should give a reasonable explanation of how the advertisement makes Belgian waffles seem fun. The answer could refer to the word "yummy" or the words "simply delicious," the cartoonish art and squiggles, the font type for the words "Belgian Waffle," or the plate of waffles shown.

Silicone Teething Beads

Question	Answer
1	C
2	B
3	soft chewy
4	The student should list how the baby is chewing on the beads and how the baby looks happy and calm rather than sore or grumpy.
5	The student should explain that babies are meant to chew on the silicone beads, which is why it is important that they are safe to chew and do not contain any harmful chemicals.
6	The student should give an opinion on whether the style of the advertisement suits the product being described. The student may have either opinion as long as it is supported by a reasonable explanation and a suitable analysis of the advertisement.

Bathroom Cleaner

Question	Answer
1	C
2	B
3	A
4	The student may list that there is no scrubbing required, that you just spray and wipe, or that the product does all the hard work.
5	The student may infer that the bubbles represent dirt, germs, odors, or stains. The answer should include a reasonable explanation of what the bubbles represent and should refer to details on the advertisement.
6	The student should identify that the picture of the bottle would most help Miss Hayden locate the product when trying to purchase it. The student could also state that the brand name would help her locate the product.

Amazing Inventions in Our Homes

Question	Answer
1	C
2	B
3	A
4	B
5	2, 1, 4, 3
6	1st
7	C
8	The student should describe how Charles Hull invented 3D printing while trying to solve the problem of how to make tabletops harder.
9	The student may list that they were too large, that they were too expensive, that they were only able to do math problems, or how they did not have the uses today like playing games or using the Internet.
10	The student should describe how the machines in the store made Charles Babbage interested in automation, and how he created his machines by trying to use automation in math.
11	The student should describe how both Babbage and Turing invented or built machines, while Grace was a programmer who developed language for computers.
12	The student should identify that all three people studied math. The student should describe how this suggests that math is necessary or important in computing.
13	The student could circle the word *excited* or the word *curious*. The student should give a reasonable justification of the choice. The answer could refer to how the author seems excited about how 3D printing could be used every day or seems curious about what the future of 3D printing might look like.
14	The student may describe how the photograph shows the small size of computers, how computers are now portable, or how computers are now used by people every day.
15	The student should give a reasonable explanation of how the history of computing shows that 3D printers may become a normal part of the home and use relevant details from the passage. The answer may refer to how having computers in the home once seemed unlikely and how computers are now used in homes every day. The answer may describe how 3D printers could become more useful, more affordable, and will eventually become common just like computers are today.

Elizabeth Blackwell – First Woman U.S. Doctor

Question	Answer
1	B
2	D
3	2, 4, 1, 3
4	B
5	A
6	inspiring, passionate
7	C
8	A
9	The student should refer to how Elizabeth's sick friend told her she wished there were female doctors because female doctors would be more caring.
10	The student should recognize that Blackwell was able to work as a doctor in Europe but not in the United States. The student should describe how this suggests that Europe was more accepting of female doctors at the time.
11	The student should describe how Blackwell opened her own doctor's office, and may also describe how she later opened her own hospital.
12	The student should relate Blackwell's actions in opening her own doctor's office or hospital to her character. The student should refer to how Blackwell took action and started her own businesses rather than waiting for someone else to employ her.
13	The student should list how Blackwell opened a medical school for women and how Blackwell was a mentor to other women wanting to become doctors.
14	The student should describe how the autobiography summarizes the changes that Blackwell's actions led to, the difference that Blackwell made, or how Blackwell made it easier for people to study medicine.
15	The student should describe how Elizabeth Blackwell opened the medical field to women. The answer may refer to how she was the first female doctor in the United States, how she opened a medical school to train female doctors, how she mentored and guided women wanting to become doctors, or how she wrote about her experiences. The student may also infer that she inspired other women, that she helped people see the good work that female doctors could do, or that she made society more accepting of female doctors.

How to Learn a New Language

Question	Answer
1	B
2	D
3	C
4	apps, videos, websites, flashcards
5	C
6	2nd and 4th
7	B
8	The student should list how you can learn more by having short practice sessions more often and how you can focus on learning just a few words a day.
9	The student should explain how the section "Practice, Practice, Practice" shows how knowing someone that is a native speaker can help you. It may refer to how you can practice with a native speaker, have a native speaker correct you, or listen to how native speakers talk.
10	The student should give a reasonable explanation of how choosing a language based on an interest in a country or culture could be motivating. The answer may refer to having a reason to learn the language or being able to plan a visit to that country.
11	The student should describe how the author explains that it takes babies three or four years to learn a language, and how adults can learn a language in half or a quarter of that time.
12	The student should list that people can lose concentration quickly and can have trouble retaining information.
13	The student should identify that both sections relate to measuring your progress and to how comparing progress can be discouraging. The answer may refer to the two sections as comparing yourself to others and comparing your own progress over time.
14	The student should give a reasonable explanation of what the word *quest* suggests. The answer could refer to *quest* as suggesting it will be challenging, will take a lot of effort, will require time and patience, or will be worth the effort.
15	The student should describe three ways people could remain positive and motivated based on the information in the passage. The answer could refer to choosing a language you really want to learn, ignoring the myths or negative ideas, not being afraid to make mistakes, not comparing yourself to others, measuring your progress, or having fun with the learning process.

It's Time for an Allowance

Question	Answer
1	C
2	B
3	B
4	A
5	A
6	The student could list learning to budget, not having to ask for money, becoming more responsible, or being able to buy things herself.
7	B
8	The student should describe the example of having to choose between spending money on snacks at school or saving the money to buy something else.
9	The student should explain that the paragraph shows that everyone needs to budget or that adults need to budget, and explain how having an allowance teaches people to budget.
10	The student should identify that the kids look positive, happy, or excited. The student should relate this to the author's idea that having an allowance would make her happier to do her chores.
11	The student may list how Frederica refers to buying things for her brothers and sisters, putting money in the poor box at church, supporting charities, or buying food for the school's food drives.
12	The student should list breaking house rules and getting bad grades.
13	The student should describe one way that the parents would benefit from Frederica having an allowance and use relevant supporting details. The answer could refer to Frederica behaving better, doing her chores more willingly, not asking for money, or not asking her mother to buy her things.
14	The student should identify that the word *nagging* suggests that the parents feel annoyed when Frederica asks for money. The student should explain that this helps show one of the benefits of Frederica having an allowance or supports the idea that having an allowance will make the family happier.
15	The student should explain how Frederica supports the idea that having an allowance would make her more responsible with money and should use relevant supporting details. The answer could refer to making smart choices about how to spend her money, learning to budget, learning to save, learning how to manage her money, or being willing to do her chores and behave well in order to earn her allowance.

The Discovery of Gold in California

Question	Answer
1	B
2	A
3	D
4	The crowds that thronged the gold regions dug up the country for miles around Sutter's mill. They tore up his beautiful valley and ruined his farm.
5	C
6	The student should complete the chart with the details below. Eggs - $1 per piece; Flour – $100 per barrel; Butcher knives – $30 each; Physician's visit – $100
7	A
8	The student should explain that Marshall was not looking for gold, but was digging a ditch for a sawmill when he accidentally discovered gold. The answer may also refer to how they were not sure it was gold at first.
9	The student should explain that Marshall was trying to work out if what he found was really gold. The answer may refer to how Marshall put vinegar on it to test it.
10	The student should describe how the author gives examples of the different types of people who came in search for gold. This included doctors, ministers, traders, mechanics, and farmers.
11	The student should list how people traveled in wagon trains over the plains and how people traveled from overseas by ship.
12	The student should identify that 80,000 Forty-niners traveled to California and compare this to the original population of California of just 10,000.
13	The student should list any four of the types of agriculture below. grain, sheep, cattle, oranges, vineyards or wine
14	The student should select one of the statements and support the choice with a reasonable explanation and relevant supporting details. The student may refer to it as being worth it because of the large amount of gold found, the size of some gold nuggets found, or the amount of money the gold was worth. The student may refer to it as not being worth it because of the hardships, because of how costly everything was, because people who found gold always wanted more, or because the gold rush only lasted a few years.
15	The student should give a reasonable summary of how the author helps show the excitement of the gold rush. The answer could refer to words and phrases used such as "half frantic" and "swarmed in," to descriptions of how people came from everywhere, or to the descriptions of the gold found.

Interview with Abraham Lincoln

Question	Answer
1	B
2	D
3	The student should explain that Cindy feels embarrassed because she made an error. The answer should refer to how she asked about playing basketball and basketball had not yet been invented.
4	A
5	The student should list Abraham, Lincoln, Mr. President, and President Lincoln.
6	A
7	D
8	The student should refer to Lincoln's answer describing how he had not studied science or engineering and show an understanding that it was impressive that he invented the device without any formal education in the area.
9	The student should list the two actions as laughing and winking. The student may infer that Lincoln is not worried that he did not study law or that he finds it amusing.
10	The student should identify that Lincoln does not enjoy fishing. The answer should refer to how he says that he does not hunt because he loves animals and then says that fish are animals too.
11	The student should explain that Lincoln corrects Cindy by saying that he does not *like* animals but *loves* them. The answer should refer to how Lincoln wants Cindy to know how much he likes animals.
12	The student should list how Lincoln's cat Tabby dined at the table with the family and how Lincoln says that his favorite animals are cats.
13	The student should explain that women being able to vote was not a popular idea at the time and not something that Lincoln thought people were ready for. The answer may also refer to Lincoln worrying that he might not be president if people knew his thoughts on the topic.
14	The student should give a reasonable description of how Lincoln looks in the photograph and relate it to how he seems in the passage. Any reasonable answer can be accepted, but possible responses could be that he looks serious, powerful, or intelligent.
15	The student should list three questions he or she would ask Abraham Lincoln and give a reasonable explanation of the reason for asking each question. The questions could be lighthearted like some of Cindy's or more serious.

Made in United States
North Haven, CT
18 April 2022

18360091R00111